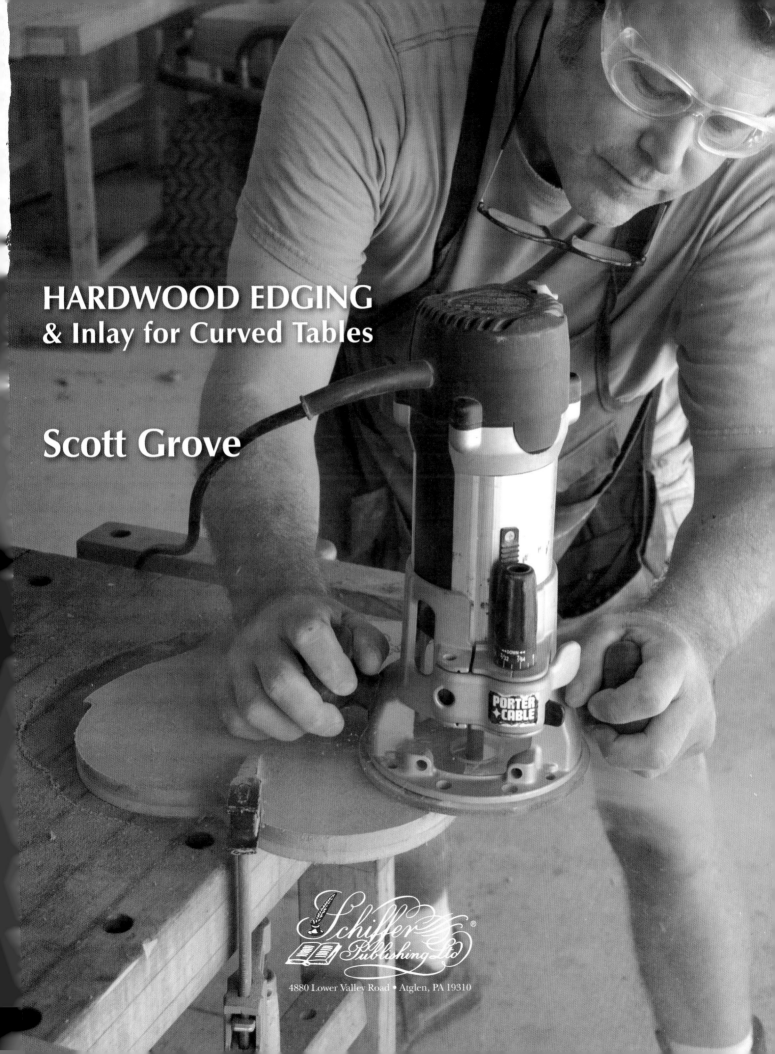

HARDWOOD EDGING
& Inlay for Curved Tables

Scott Grove

Schiffer Publishing Ltd

4880 Lower Valley Road • Atglen, PA 19310

Other Schiffer Books
by Scott Grove

Advanced Veneering and
Alternative Techniques
ISBN 978-0-7643-3846-5

Other Schiffer Books
on Related Subjects

Creating a Fine Art Entry
Table, Robert Ortiz
ISBN 978-0-7643-3071-1

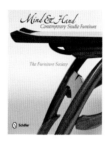

Mind & Hand: Contemporary
Studio Furniture, The
Furniture Society
ISBN 978-0-7643-4115-1

Mission Furniture: How to
Make It, H. H. Windsor
ISBN 978-0-7643-2835-0

Type set in Zapf Humnst BT
ISBN: 978-0-7643-5118-1

Printed in China

Published by Schiffer Publishing, Ltd.
4880 Lower Valley Road
Atglen, PA 19310
Phone: (610) 593-1777; Fax: (610) 593-2002
E-mail: Info@schifferbooks.com
Web: www.schifferbooks.com

For our complete selection of fine books on this and related
subjects, please visit our website at www.schifferbooks.com.
You may also write for a free catalog.

Schiffer Publishing's titles are available at special discounts
for bulk purchases for sales promotions or premiums. Special
editions, including personalized covers, corporate imprints,
and excerpts, can be created in large quantities for special
needs. For more information, contact the publisher.

We are always looking for people to write books on new
and related subjects. If you have an idea for a book, please
contact us at proposals@schifferbooks.com.

Dedication

I dedicate this book to my mother, Patricia A. Grove, who always inspired me, and to my amazing sons, Zee and Shu (Zach and Sean). I love you.

Acknowledgments

I would like to thank Michael Fortune; Marc Adams and the Marc Adams School of Woodworking; Anselm Fraser and the Chippendale International School of Woodworking; Greg Znajda, George Neireiter, and Graham Burbank for their encouragement. Special thanks to Nancy Napurski, my Lionheart, for her editing skills and continuing support.

Contents

Foreword

I've known and worked with Scott Grove for many years; he is a talented craftsman and teacher.

His ability to see, break down, and describe complex operations into understandable steps is remarkable, and his students come away with new skills that allow them to create higher levels of work—impeccable craftsmanship, learned at a fast pace.

With this book, Scott has transformed the sometimes difficult task of adding a curved hardwood edge into easy-to-follow steps. He describes many nuances and alternate methods in detail along the way, as well as how to create homemade jigs and low-budget solutions for many of the processes.

The illustrated summary on page 92 is a great map and reference guide, and with many visual aids from photographs, drawings, and 3-D renderings, he depicts each step clearly.

This book is a must-have for professionals and hobbyist woodworkers alike; it reveals many secrets and clears up all the gray areas for how to apply a hardwood edge and inlay to any type of curved table edge.

I look forward to seeing how it impacts the woodworking field and broadens the possibilities.
— Michael C. Fortune, world-renowned master craftsman and member of the Royal Canadian Academy of Art

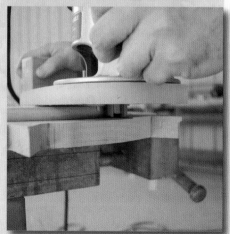

Introduction

Applying a hardwood edge to an organic or complex curved table can be a challenge. When the curve is a French or serpentine curve, it can be a test of patience and craftsmanship to precisely match up the hardwood to the table edge.

This book shows you how to apply a hardwood edge to a curved tabletop edge using a set of large, offset template guides installed on a router base that, when used properly, will accurately match a hardwood edge to any curve. This template system also lets you cut seam inlays quickly and cut perfect, parallel outside edges that match an inner seam.

I initially developed this system for an oval demilune table that had a graceful French curve. A French curve is not a simple, one-dimensional radius; the radius slowly transitions, so I couldn't use a simple single-axis, one-length radius swing arm on my router to cut the curve. The technique I devised allows me to mate the French curve with a hardwood edge perfectly.

Since then I have used it for various complex curves, large and small, graceful and squiggly. In this book, I demonstrate the system on a small, asymmetrical, heart-shaped table, which illustrates most of the variations that the system can perform. I also use a few of my students' projects to illustrate odd details and quirky alternatives. I hope you enjoy it.

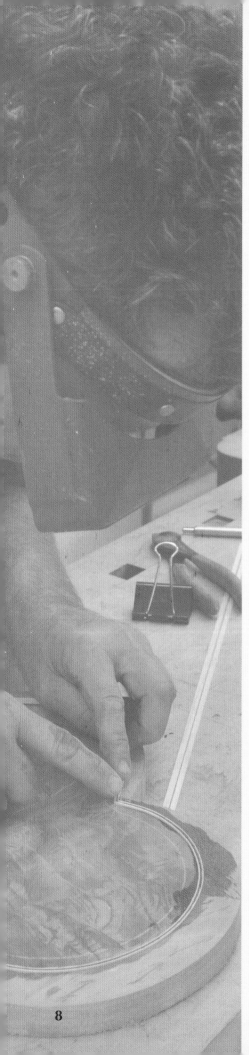

1.
Overview

In brief, this system uses templates and template guides on a router, which allows you to cut on either side of the table field and hardwood edge seam. The same template is used to cut an inlay directly centered on the seam as well as to cut the outside edge parallel to the seam. Once set up, edging can be applied to any curve quickly and precisely.

There are many ways to sequence this system of templates. I have broken down the steps for easier comprehension; on the first try, I suggest you follow the longer version (steps 1–8). Once you have a good understanding of the concept, you can use the shorter version by combining or rearranging a few steps and overlapping the cuts to speed up the process. I have illustrated a few variations at the end of the book.

I have also included important alternate steps along the way. Whether or not you use these depends on a number of factors, such as the complexity of the curve and the size of the table, to name only a few examples.

Understanding the components and their names can be a challenge, and at first it might be confusing—but have faith and hang in there. Once you get through the process a light will go on and you'll be an expert.

To start, make sure you have the proper tools in your shop (see chapter 6). There are a variety of alternate tools and methods you can use, as demonstrated throughout.

Before continuing, I suggest you review the glossary to familiarize yourself with terminology. Here are the most important terms:

Table: the finished piece, which consists of the veneered portion and the hardwood edge.

Master pattern: the first full-scale template of your table without the hardwood edge.

Field: the veneered portion of the table without the hardwood edge. This is the exact size of the master pattern.

Seam: the seam between the hardwood edge and the veneered field.

ID template: the inner dimension template, ½″ smaller than the field on all sides.

OD template: the outer dimension template, ½″ larger than the field on all sides.

Butt joint: the end grain seam or joint between two hardwood edging pieces.

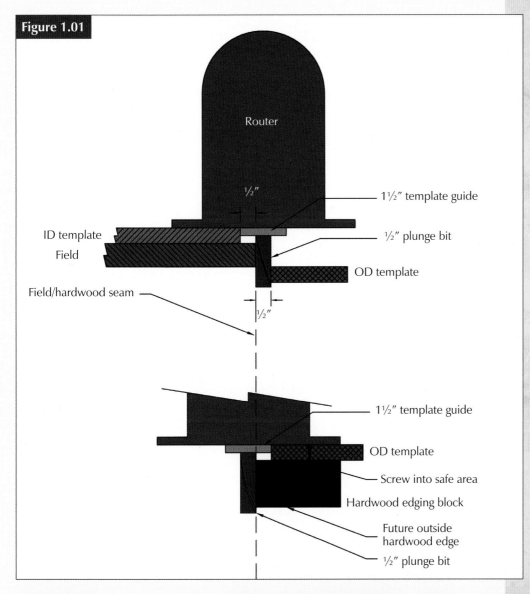

Figure 1.01

Router

1½" template guide

½" plunge bit

ID template

Field

OD template

Field/hardwood seam

½"

½"

1½" template guide

OD template

Screw into safe area

Hardwood edging block

Future outside
hardwood edge

½" plunge bit

Figure 1.01. Notice how
the router bit is shifted to
either side of the field/
hardwood seam.

Figure 1.02. Three main
components: ID template,
field, and OD template.
Notice the OD template is
a doughnut shape, with 3"
of material on the outside
for structure.

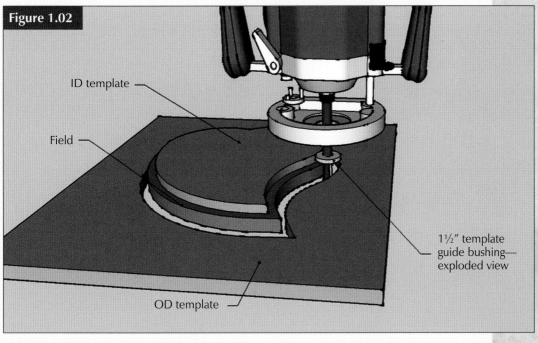

Figure 1.02

ID template

Field

1½" template
guide bushing—
exploded view

OD template

2.
Drawing the Table Shape

First you need to design your table shape. I like to roughly sketch out my concept and work out the size and proportions of the overall table. For the example in this book, it is a small, heart-shaped table with a key design within the veneer pattern representing the "key to my heart." (There's nothing like making an anniversary present while writing a book.) I sketch out the concept and refine it to the exact shape and size of the final table. Having smooth transition curves is the secret for a successful shape. Here's how to do it:

First, sketch your full-scale table shape freehand. It can be an arbitrary organic form or a graceful French curved oval, or the shape can relate to a veneer design, as in this heart-shaped example. Draw the entire table, including the veneered field and hardwood edging. The edge may be parallel to the seam or vary in width.

Your drawing can be created on paper before any veneer is laid up. For this example, I already have my veneer design ready to go. I also did not sketch on the outside of the hardwood edge, as in this case I know I want to intuitively resolve the outside perimeter at the very end. (I don't always practice what I preach.) If you are a beginner, sketch out the field and hardwood edge.

Figure 2.01. Since my veneer is taped on the front/side facing up, I cannot accurately locate the center "key" design element, so I roughly sketch out my table shape on the back side of the veneer.

Figure 2.02. The chalk line represents the size and shape of the table field, not the outside hardwood edging. The table field is the table minus the hardwood edge.

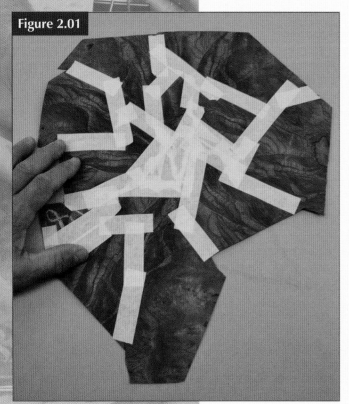

Figure 2.01

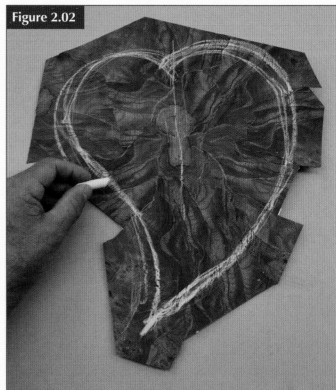

Figure 2.02

10

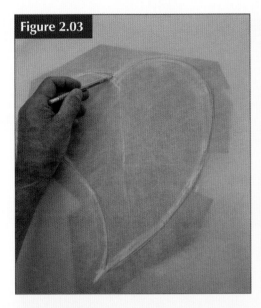

Figure 2.03

Figure 2.04

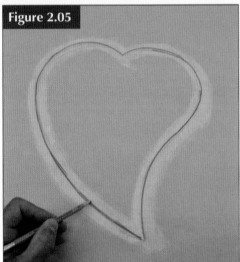

Figure 2.05

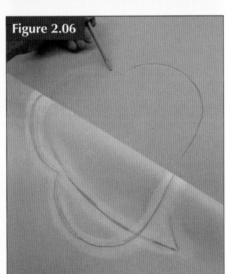

Figure 2.06

Figure 2.03. Since the top, or face side, of the veneer is taped and I want to see and center the design in my tabletop, I sketch out the table shape again in reverse on tracing paper.

Figure 2.04. The reversed table shape is then transferred to a sheet of ½" MDF, right side up, which becomes my first template, the master pattern. To do this, sketch out the table shape on a piece of tracing paper with the veneer design under it as your shape reference. Then trace the sketched line with white chalk.

Figures 2.05–2.06. Flip the tracing paper over, place it on a piece of ½" MDF, and redraw over the original line. This transfers the chalk onto the MDF. Then, darken the white line with a pencil. This becomes the master pattern and represents the shape of the field without the hardwood edge. For beginners, I recommend also sketching the very outside edge of the table to include the hardwood edge.

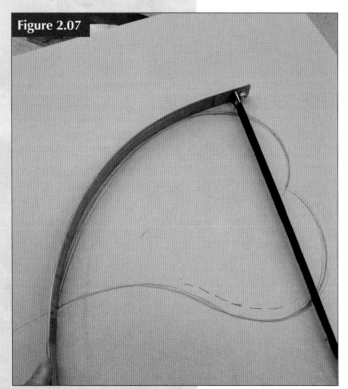

Figure 2.07

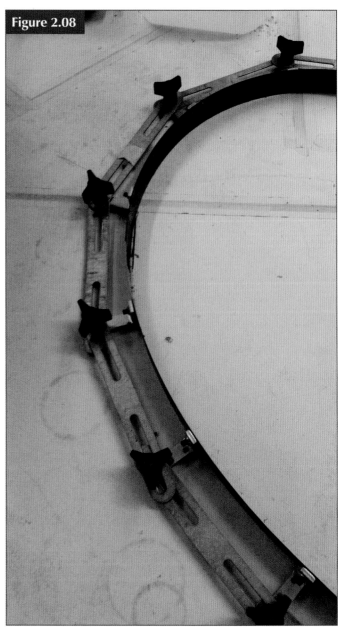

Figure 2.08

Figures 2.07–2.08. I like to use a tapered asymmetrical drawing bow (available from LeeValley.com) to draw the smooth transitioning French curve portion of the heart; an adjustable curve drawing guide works well, too.

I now have a rough sketch that needs to be cleaned up and refined. This step can be performed on a computer using a rendering or CAD program, but printing large, full-scale drawings can be inconvenient and costly. I typically draw them by hand, using various tools to refine the shape.

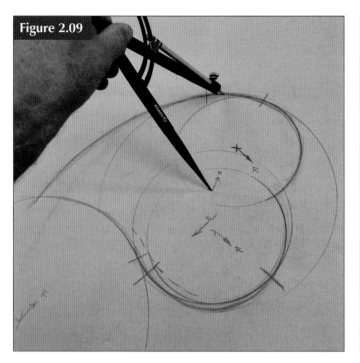

Figure 2.09

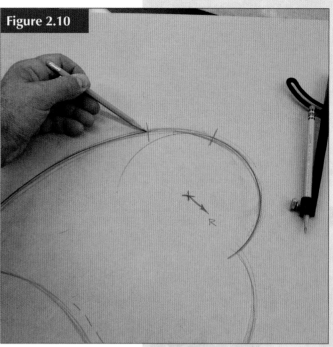

Figure 2.10

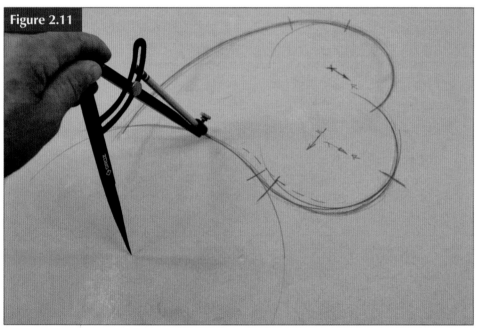

Figure 2.11

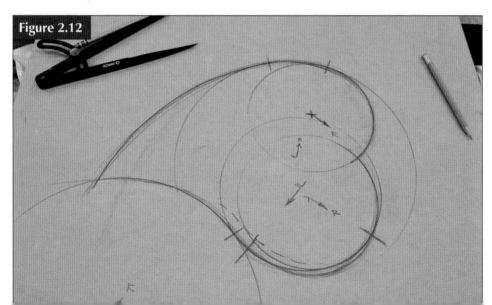

Figure 2.12

Figures 2.09–2.10. I use a standard compass to locate the areas that have a simple radius. This takes a bit of trial and error to find the center point. When it is located, mark it and the tangent intersection areas with a perpendicular line. This identifies sections that will need to be perfectly transitioned and smoothed (sanded) in the following steps.

Figures 2.11–2.12. With my compass, I work my way around the shape, drawing in all the curves, ensuring that the transition, or tangent, from one curve to another lines up smoothly. The above steps can be drawn simply by hand, but the key is that the curves should transition smoothly.

Important: Keep in mind that this drawing will become your master pattern from which all other templates are made, so it needs to be perfect.

3.
Templates

Step 1. Master Pattern

This system relies on a series of templates for the router to follow when you cut the various parts. Take your time to create this first one. Once the shape has been drawn and refined, cut it out.

Figures 3.01–3.02. Use a band saw or jigsaw to roughly cut the shape just outside the line (shown).

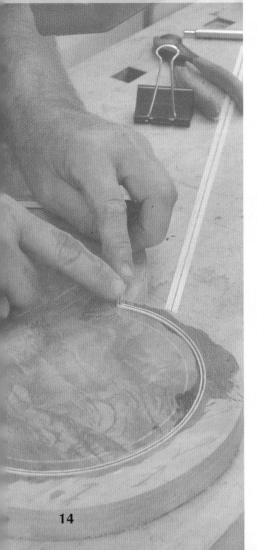

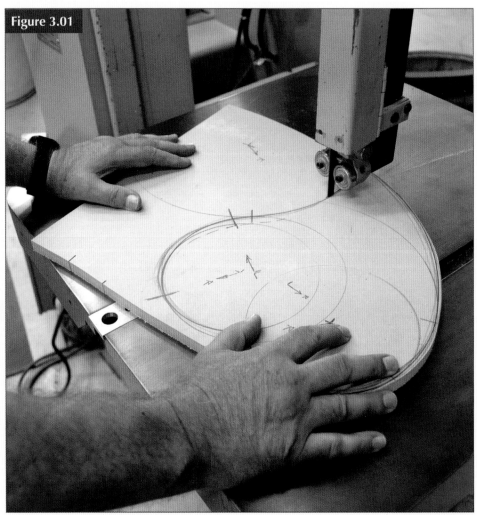

Figure 3.01

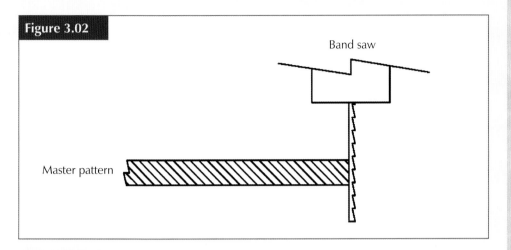

Figure 3.02

Band saw

Master pattern

Figure 3.03. The outside hardwood edge can be parallel, tapered, or a combination of the two.

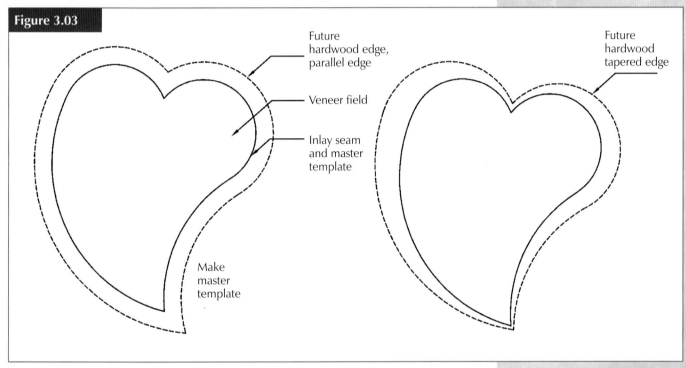

Figure 3.03

Future hardwood edge, parallel edge

Veneer field

Inlay seam and master template

Make master template

Future hardwood tapered edge

Figure 3.04

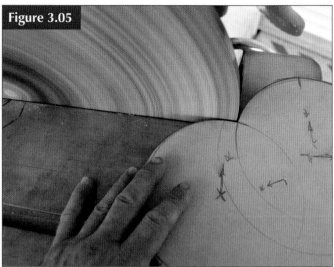

Figure 3.05

Figures 3.04–3.05. Then sand precisely to the line, keeping the curves smooth and transitional. It's important to make light, gentle passes and keep the part moving to avoid creating flat spots.

Figure 3.06. Use a spindle sander for inside curves, which are the hardest areas to do. I use the largest diameter drum available and make light passes. On large tables I use a hand-held belt sander.

Figure 3.07. Once you've sanded to the line and it looks good, feel the curve, especially the transition areas from one radius to another. Stroke the curve quickly back and forth with your finger and mark the spots that feel high and low. I use arrows for high spots and a downward curve for low spots.

Figure 3.06

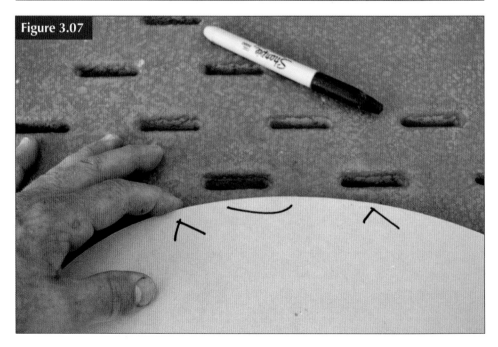

Figure 3.07

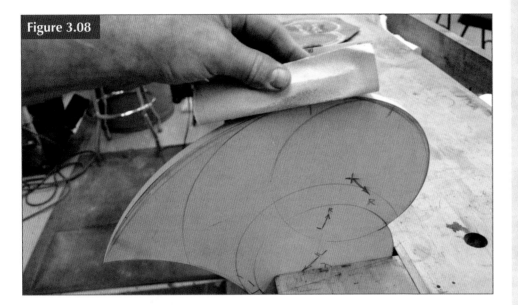

Figure 3.08

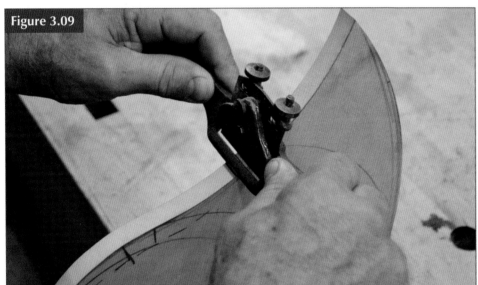

Figure 3.09

Figures 3.08–3.09. Work out these subtle bumps by hand with a spokeshave or file and finish with sandpaper on a hard sanding block.

Figure 3.10. This master pattern represents the exact shape of the field: note that the template barely fits onto the veneer. That's okay—as long as the veneer extends past the master pattern even a tiny bit, we're good. I typically like to shoot for a 1″ wider veneer field.

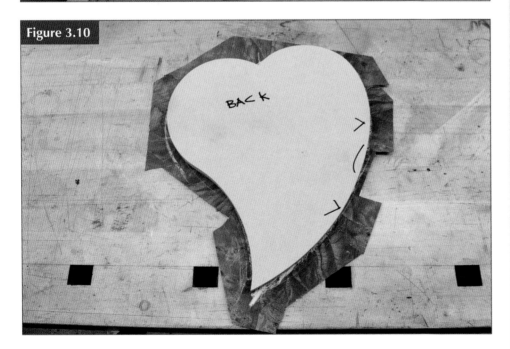

Figure 3.10

BACK

Figures 3.11–3.12. Trace the master pattern onto ½″ MDF, then saw close to the outside edge first on a band saw or jigsaw, which helps reduce dust and strain on the router when performing the next step.

Figure 3.13. Using a flush trim router bit, create a duplicate of the master pattern.

Step 2. Duplicate Master Pattern

If you are planning to add an inlay to the seam and any of the edges are sharply curved, make a duplicate master pattern out of ½″ MDF using a flush trim bit. This second pattern will be used for pre-bending the inlay. It will also help with hand work in later steps and must be an exact duplicate.

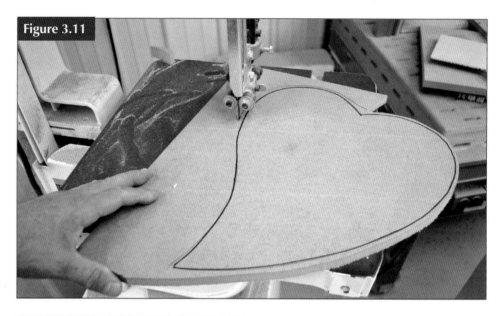

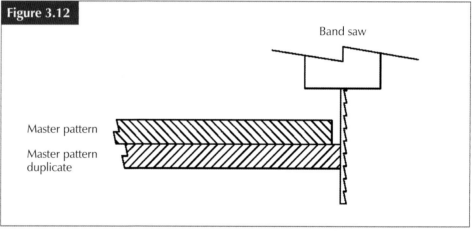

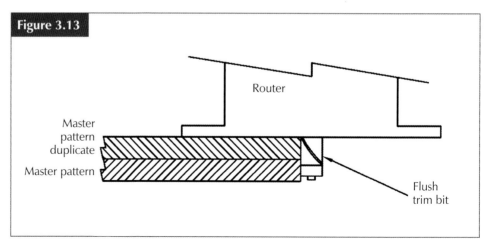

Step 3. ID Template

Create the ID template by reducing the master pattern size by ½″ measured by hand or with a router as described in the following pages.

Once you understand the entire process you will be able to determine if hand drawing is acceptable or not. I prefer to use a ½″ rabbeting router bit to reduce the pattern exactly.

Figure 3.14

Figure 3.14. To reduce the master pattern by ½″, you can redraw the shape using dividers to shrink it and re-cut. This is okay for a loose interpretation of the original shape and works fine for this type of design.

Figures 3.15–3.17. For a more accurate size reduction, use a router with a ½″ rabbeting bit and cut ¼″ down into the ½″ MDF all the way around, then remove the remaining lip with a flush trip bit.

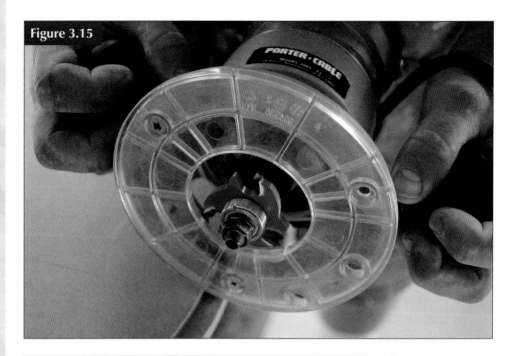

Figure 3.15

Figure 3.16

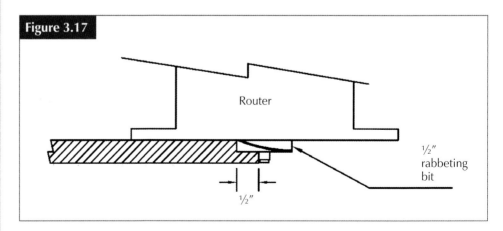

Figure 3.17

Router

½″ rabbeting bit

½″

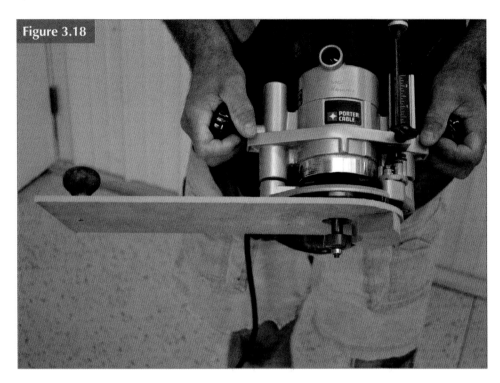

Figure 3.18.

Figure 3.18. During the cutting process, there might be some areas, like sharp outside corners (or in my table, the bottom of the heart), where the router base does not have much surface contact on the master pattern. It is important to have a steady hand and be aware of the stability of the router. An extended router base and/or a steady rest block is good insurance for these areas.

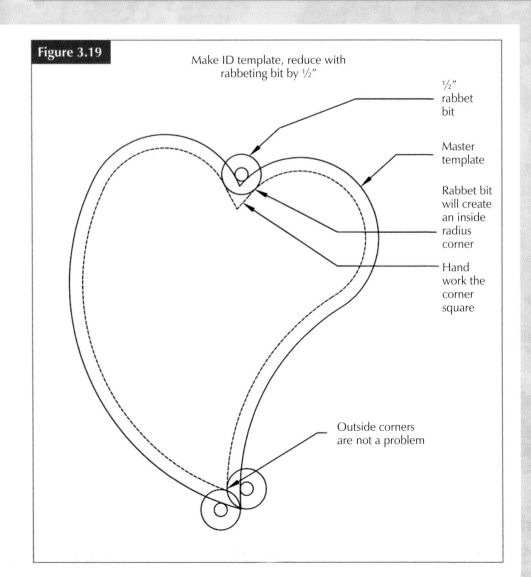

Figure 3.19

Make ID template, reduce with rabbeting bit by ½"

½" rabbet bit

Master template

Rabbet bit will create an inside radius corner

Hand work the corner square

Outside corners are not a problem

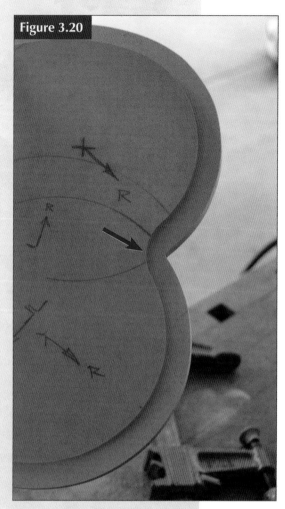

Figure 3.20

Figure 3.21

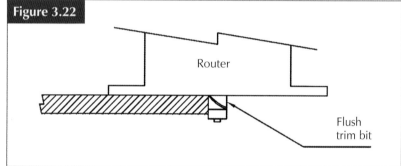

Figure 3.22

Router

Flush trim bit

Figure 3.20. Inside corners will have a radius created by the rabbeting bit. In the next step you will cut off the remaining lip and this inside radius will need to be sharpened by hand.

Figures 3.21–3.23. Now with a flush trim bit (bottom bearing), flip the pattern over and router the remaining rabbet lip flush.

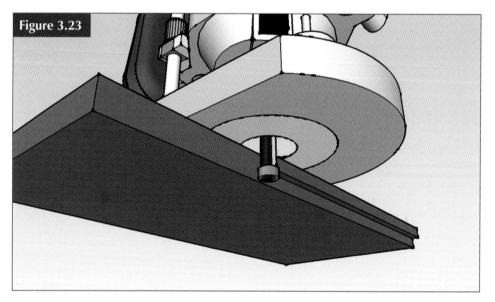

Figure 3.23

Figure 3.24

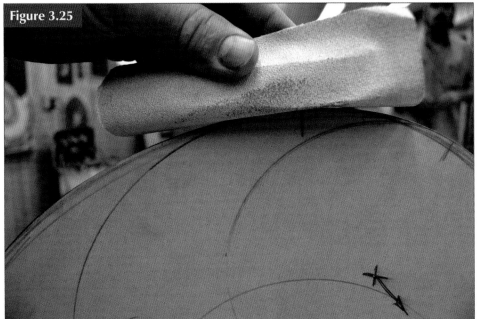

Figure 3.25

Figure 3.24. An alternative and safer way to make this cut is to use a router table. To avoid excessive dust and wear and tear on the router and bit, saw away the waste close to the edge of the template prior to routing (not shown).

Figure 3.25. Lightly sand any ridge that may be left from the two machining steps.

Figures 3.26–3.27. This is your ID template. Now attach it to a larger ¾" piece of MDF (or desired thickness of your table field) with good-quality double-stick tape, with at least 3" of clearance around the entire shape. This extra 3" of material will provide support for a steady rest mounted on the router when you cut the field. Or if you use an extended router base, the ¾" MDF will need to extend only ¾" past the ID template.

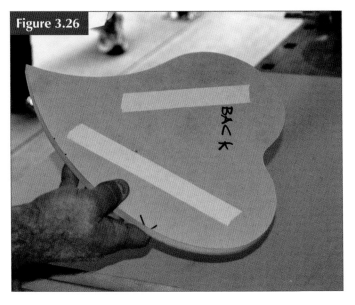

Figure 3.26

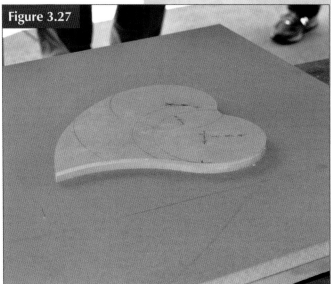

Figure 3.27

Step 4. Cutting the Field

Now we cut out the field using the ID template. The field can be either veneered first or can be just a core material such as MDF or flake board. I prefer MDF.

This step requires a minimum 1½ plunge router with a 1½″ OD template guide and a ½″ plunge cut router bit. I have not found a stock-manufactured 1½″ template guide or bushing, so I had one made.

The one shown here was made by a machinist out of ¼″ aluminum sheet stock with an ID (inner dimension) of ⅝″ to friction-fit over a stock, store-bought ⅝″ OD template guide. I also had others laser cut out of ¼″ acrylic and turned them myself from phenolic and wood. In a pinch, I have even made one of ¼″ MDF and simply sanded the circular guide on a disc sander.

See page 68 on how to create a simple jig to quickly and accurately make any size template guide bushing required in this book.

Figures 3.28–3.29. My custom-machined bushing with a store-bought ⅝″ template guide is installed on my router base. To clarify, I made a 1½″ bushing that fit over a store-bought template guide and call this assembly a "template guide."

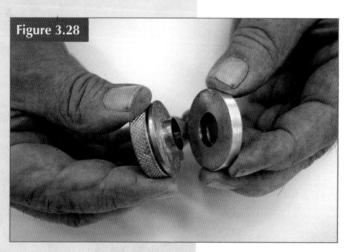

Figure 3.28

Figure 3.29

Obviously, the more accurate the template guide assembly, the better, but it isn't that critical—all of the above mentioned bushings work just fine. One reason is that most store-bought template guides don't fit the router bases exactly. There is usually a little wiggle, but in most cases this is not a problem because the wood edging flexes during clamping and will easily compensate for slight misalignment in the template guide.

One exception is if you are installing a very thin inlay over the seam, say ¹/₁₆″ of stringing, and wish to use this template system to cut the inlay groove. Then higher tolerances are required, and you can use a centering pin or cone to center the template guide exactly to the router bit.

Figures 3.30–3.31. A centering cone or centering pin will align the template guide on the router base perfectly with the router bit. The cone is shown with a 1½″ bushing, the pin with a 3″ bushing, which will be explained later.

Figure 3.30

Figure 3.31

Figure 3.32

Figure 3.33

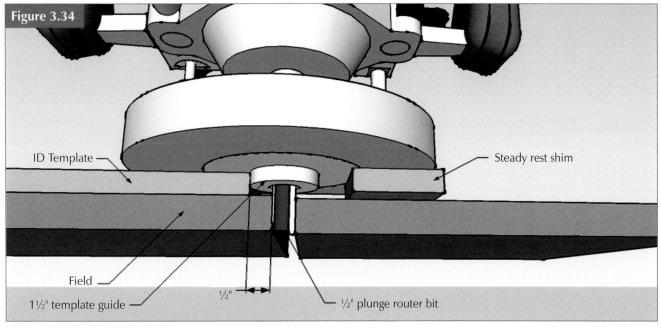

Figure 3.34

ID Template

Steady rest shim

Field

1½" template guide

½"

½" plunge router bit

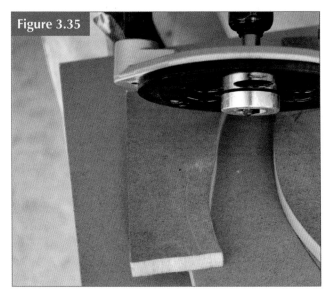

Figure 3.35

Figures 3.32–3.34. If I'm not using an extended router base, I like to add a steady rest block on one side of the router base bottom. This provides extra support during cutting and keeps the router base flat on the cutting surface. To make one, simply attach a small, ½" block of MDF (or use the same thickness of the primary template) with double-stick tape, or use super-glue (CA glue) to attach it to one side of the router base.

Figure 3.35. In lieu of attaching a steady rest to the router base, you can use scraps from rough-cutting out the ID template to help support the router base. Fasten them to the field perimeter using double-stick tape.

STOP! READ THIS!
Outside Corners and the No-Cut Zone

Tables with outside corners require additional steps. Before routing—cutting out the field—it is vital that you understand this next concept.

When using the ID template to cut out the field, outside corners become rounded corners. So, when your design has outside angled corners, you need to take precautions to prevent damaging the field. In other words, the template guide rolls around an outside corner on the ID template and creates a radius corner on the field, which you don't want (see fig. 3.44 on page 29).

To prevent rounding these corners, mark them on the ID template as no-cut areas. In addition, mark any outside curve that is less than a ¾" radius as a no-cut area. These corners and tight outside radii will have to be worked after routing out the majority of the field.

Using the duplicate master pattern and a flush trim router bit will help you cut these angled outside corners. Any inside corners will yield a radius and will need to be hand worked as well. This is an important concept to understand, as this process repeats throughout.

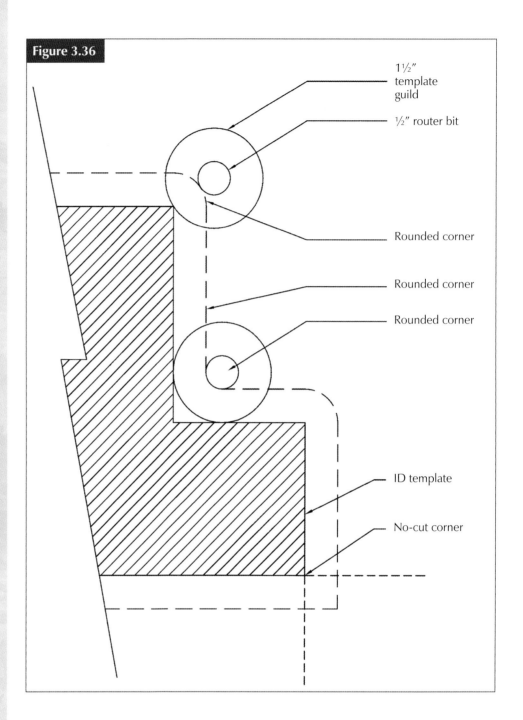

Figure 3.36

1½" template guild

½" router bit

Rounded corner

Rounded corner

Rounded corner

ID template

No-cut corner

Figure 3.36. Note the rounded outside and inside corners created if you router around a square template corner. The inside corner can't be avoided and is not a problem. The outside corner will cut off material you need, so mark the template with no-cut areas.

Figure 3.37

Figure 3.38

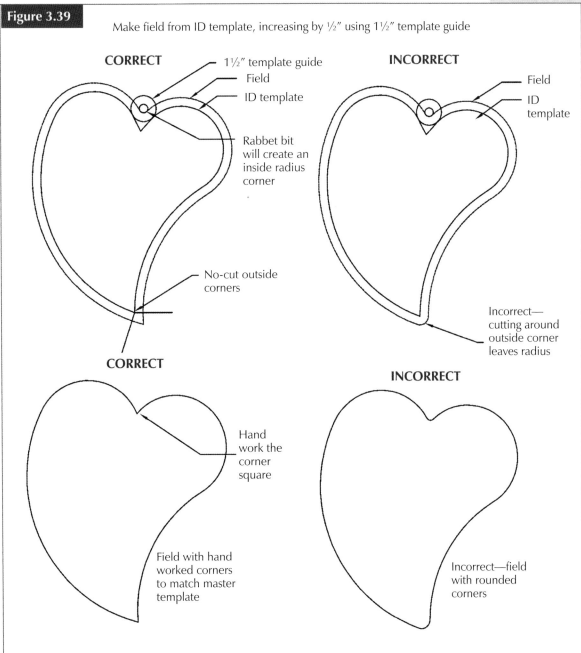

Figure 3.39

Make field from ID template, increasing by ½″ using 1½″ template guide

CORRECT

1½″ template guide

Field

ID template

Rabbet bit will create an inside radius corner

No-cut outside corners

INCORRECT

Field

ID template

Incorrect—cutting around outside corner leaves radius

CORRECT

Hand work the corner square

Field with hand worked corners to match master template

INCORRECT

Incorrect—field with rounded corners

Figures 3.37–3.39. Make a plunge-cut roughly ⅛″ to ¼″ deep into the MDF field. This field is under the ID template and needs to be saved, so it's not a problem if you stray outside the line.

27

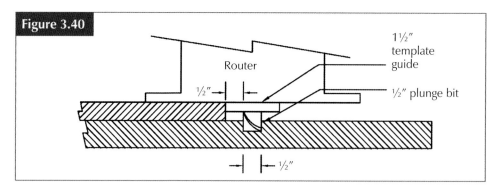

Figure 3.40

Router   1½" template guide

½"   ½" plunge bit

½"

Figures 3.40–3.42.
Remember: do not cut around outside corners and curves less than ¾" radius. If you do, it will round the corner of the field and remove material you want to keep. I like to mark my ID template beforehand to remind me while I am cutting.

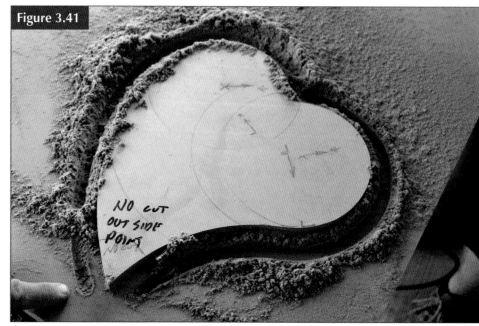

Figure 3.41

Figure 3.42

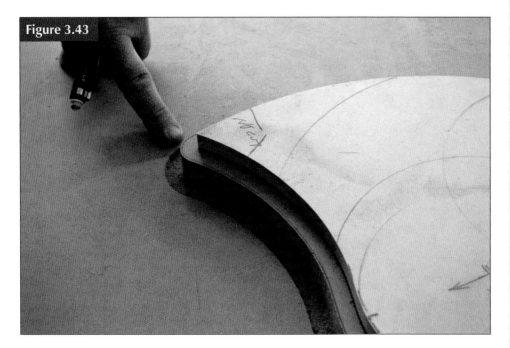

Figure 3.43

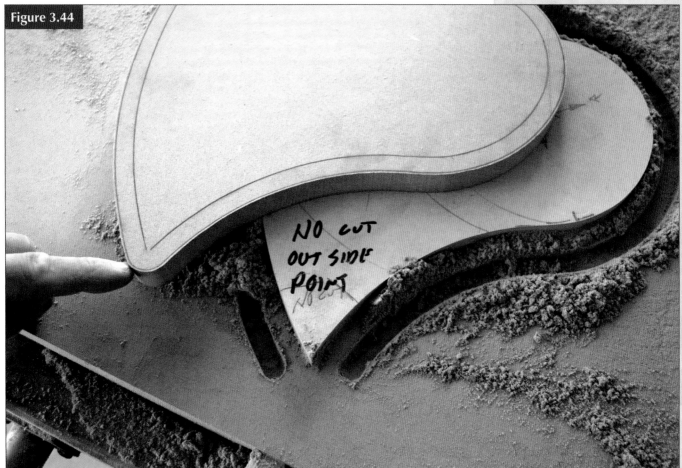

Figure 3.44

NO CUT
OUT SIDE
POINT

Figures 3.43–3.44.
I intentionally routed around the ID template corner. Note how the field tip is rounded—it should be pointed.

Figures 3.45–3.47. Cut out the field shape with a band saw (shown) or jigsaw. This does not have to be an accurate cut; simply stay within the routed kerf. (A kerf is the groove, or void, left by a cutting tool.)

Figure 3.45

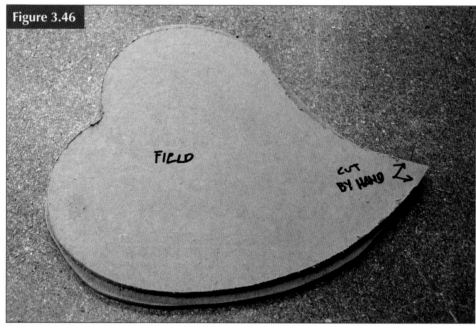

Figure 3.46

FIELD

CUT BY HAND

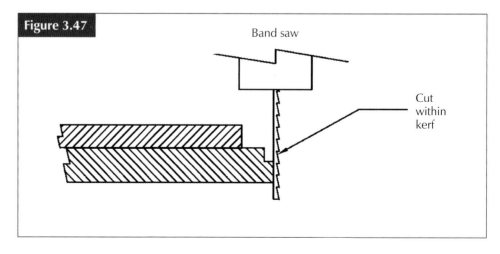

Figure 3.47

Band saw

Cut within kerf

Figure 3.48

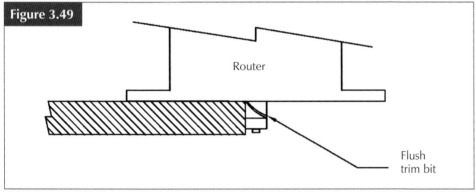

Figure 3.49

Router

Flush
trim bit

Figures 3.48–3.49. Flip the piece over so the tongue or lip is up, and then remove the lip with a flush trim router bit with a bottom bearing.

Figure 3.50. Again, a router table makes this step easier.

Figure 3.50

Figure 3.51

Figures 3.51–3.52. For the no-cut corners, you can use the master template or simply extend the curve visually and sand the outside corner by hand with an edge or disc sander. It is important to keep the edge square. That said, I don't like to use a handheld belt sander for this step unless it is mounted to a table with a square fence.

Figure 3.52

Figure 3.53

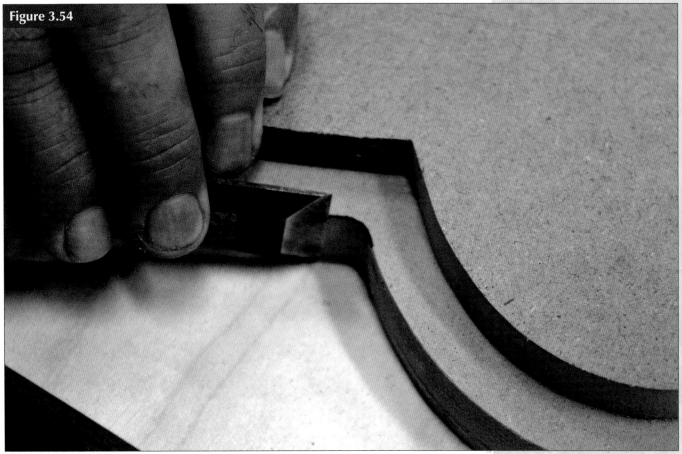

Figure 3.54

Figures 3.53–3.54. The inside corners can now be sharpened by hand or on a sander. In this example the field was veneered beforehand, but I prefer veneering afterward to avoid the risk of damaging the veneer.

Note: Since the template guide is riding on the inside (the ID template) and the cutter is cutting on the outside, it is easy for the router to shudder and skip off the ID template and cut farther into outside material, which is the "good" side. If this happens, no worries; it can be repaired. Be sure to start your cut with the guide tight to the ID template. See Template Repair on page 39.

Figures 3.55–3.56. Cut the OD template with a plunge router, keeping the router guide tight to the ID template. A steady rest or extended base (not shown) can be used for stability.

Step 5. Cutting the OD Template

You now have the finished field—the table top that will receive the hardwood edge. This field can be veneered before or after the above cutting process. To create the OD template, repeat step 4 on page 24, but this time you can ignore the no-cut areas and simply cut all the way around the ID template.

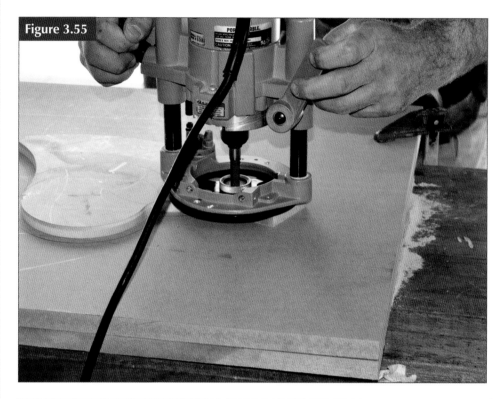

Figure 3.55

Figure 3.56

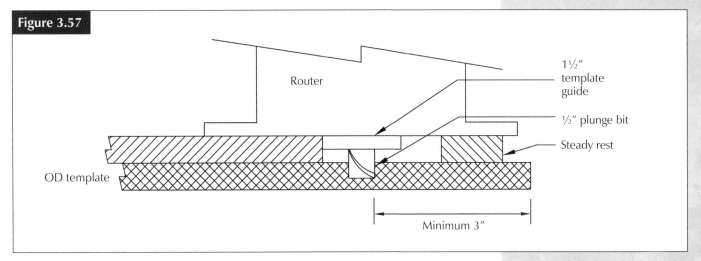

Figure 3.57

Router

1½" template guide

½" plunge bit

Steady rest

OD template

Minimum 3"

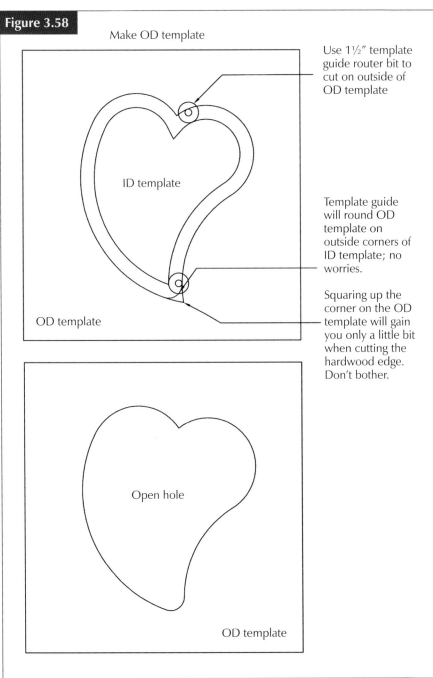

Figure 3.58

Make OD template

Use 1½" template guide router bit to cut on outside of OD template

ID template

Template guide will round OD template on outside corners of ID template; no worries.

Squaring up the corner on the OD template will gain you only a little bit when cutting the hardwood edge. Don't bother.

OD template

Open hole

OD template

Figures 3.57–3.58. The ID template is used to cut the OD template, cutting only halfway down into the MDF. Be sure to leave at least 3" of material on the outside for structure on the final OD template. You can cut all the way through the OD template, but you will need a spoiler board under it to avoid cutting into your work bench.

35

Figure 3.59–3.60. After drilling a hole in the kerf, cut out the center of the OD template with a jigsaw, staying inside the kerf.

Figure 3.59

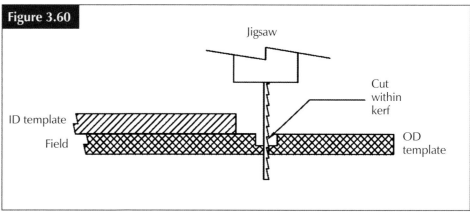

Figure 3.60

Figure 3.61

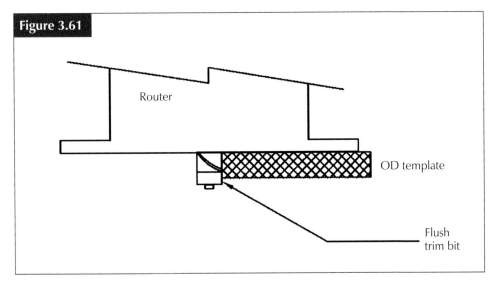

Router

OD template

Flush
trim bit

Figure 3.61. After cutting out
the inside waste portion,
remove and flush the edge
with a flush trim bit.

Figure 3.62. The field and the
OD template: Notice the
bottom tip of the heart is
rounded on the OD template,
created by rolling around the
corner. This is not a problem:
the hardwood edge will be
hand worked during the final
fitting in this area.

Figure 3.62

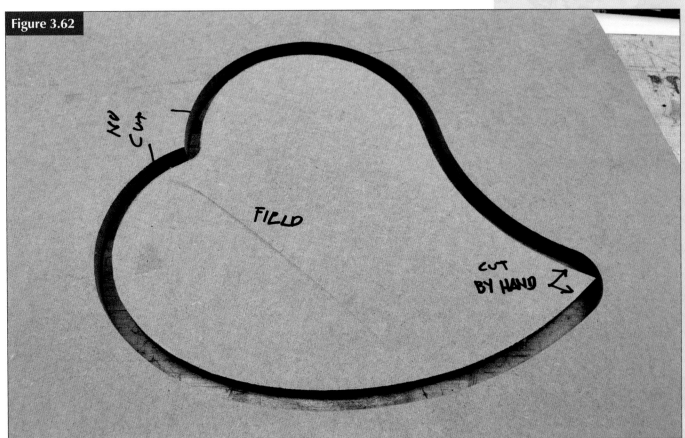

NO CUT

FIELD

CUT
BY HAND

Alternate: Combine Steps 4 and 5

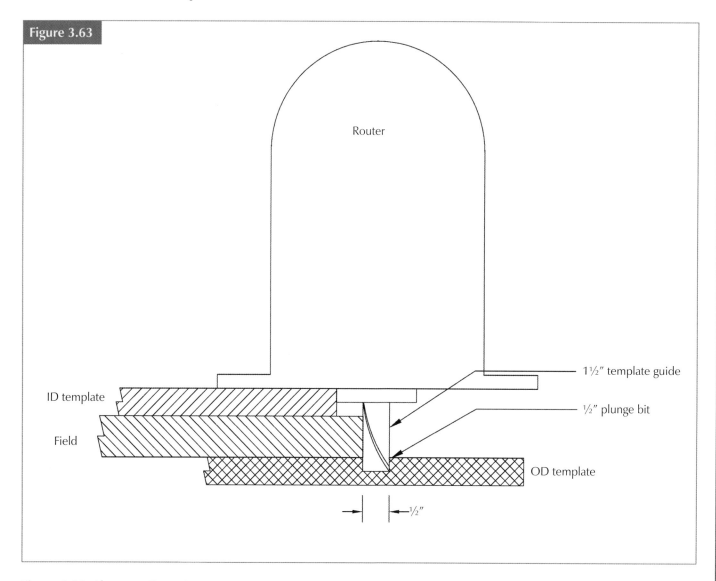

Figure 3.63

Router

1½" template guide

ID template

½" plunge bit

Field

OD template

½"

Figure 3.63. Alternate: Steps 4 and 5 are often combined to cut the field and OD template at the same time. The OD template acts as a spoiler board, too. I have separated them into a long version for easier understanding of each step.

Figure 3.64. The ID template, field (under the ID template), and OD template. Each is ½" larger than the previous.

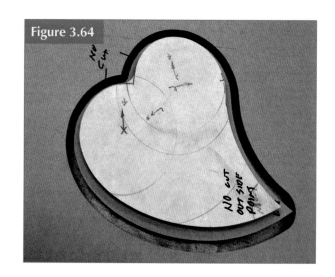

Figure 3.64

Template Repair

Figure 3.65

Figure 3.65. A steady hand is required when cutting the outside template because your router template guide is following an inside template and cutting on the outside. With this scenario, the router might wiggle and cut into the outside template. No worries—it can be repaired.

Figure 3.66

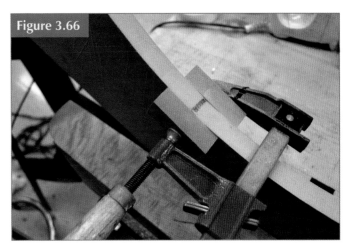

Figure 3.66. To repair this, wrap cellophane tape around some scrap material (to prevent the automotive putty from sticking to it), clamp them on either side, and leave the edge proud of the finished curve.

Figure 3.67

Figure 3.68

Figures 3.67–3.68. Mix a little automotive putty or Bondo to fill the void. Sand flush when the putty sets up in five to ten minutes.

4.
Hardwood Edge

Step 6. Cutting the Hardwood Seam

Here is where it all comes together. You will be using the OD template to guide the router in cutting the hardwood's inside edge to perfectly match the field, making a nice, tight seam.

First, determine how many hardwood edge sections there are and where the butt joints will meet. I use the ID template to help visualize these and mark the joints directly on both the ID and OD template.

A number of factors affect the layout and selection of the hardwood edge. The primary issues are the tightness of the curves on the table and how much exposed end grain on the hardwood edge is aesthetically acceptable. The tighter the curve and the longer the board, the more end grain is exposed.

Another consideration is the available width of the stock lumber: the wider the board, the tighter the radius can be achieved with one board. A tighter radius means more exposed end grain. Typically, the tighter the radius, the shorter the sections and less end grain will be exposed. I prefer not to exceed 45 degrees of end grain running off the side of the edging.

Figure 4.01

Left figure labels: 3", 44°, Exposed endgrain, 12", 10¾", 6½" R, 1" curved edging, Wood blank, 1"

Right figure labels: 2", 25°, Exposed endgrain, 12", 9¼", R9", 1" curved edging, Wood blank, 1"

Figure 4.02

Figure 4.03

Continuous Edging

This template system also works for fitting steam-bent and laminated edging, which eliminates the exposed end grain issue and minimizes the number of butt joints.

Figure 4.02. Note the curved table edge is one laminated board.

Figure 4.03. Steam-bent edging.

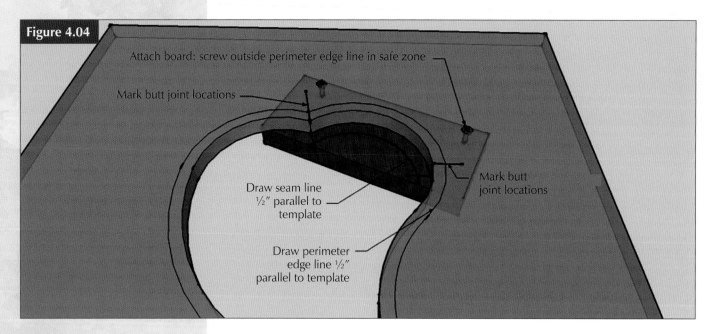

Figure 4.04

Attach board: screw outside perimeter edge line in safe zone

Mark butt joint locations

Draw seam line ½" parallel to template

Draw perimeter edge line ½" parallel to template

Mark butt joint locations

Figure 4.04. For applying a 1"-wide hardwood edge, draw an additional line, the "perimeter edge," ½" around the entire OD template. This represents the outside cut of the hardwood edging. If you want a wider edge, or if it varies in width, lay it out on the OD template by referencing the master drawing.

Beyond this perimeter edge, there is a "safe zone" that allows you to screw the hardwood to the OD template without damaging the finished hardwood edge.

Once you determine the edging butt joint locations (where the two hardwood edges come together end to end), transfer them from the ID to the OD template.

Figure 4.05. Slide the edging board blank under the OD template and align so it fits roughly between the butt joint lines. Leave at least ½" additional material inside the OD template. Hold it in place temporarily with a clamp, or screw the board in the safe zone, outside the perimeter edge.

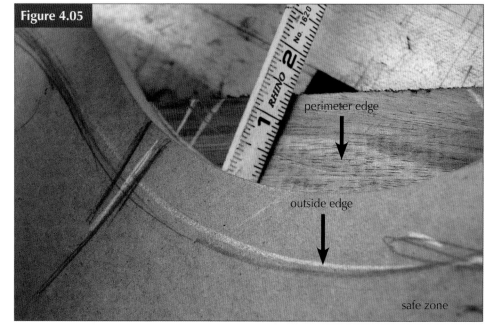

Figure 4.05

perimeter edge

outside edge

safe zone

Figure 4.06.

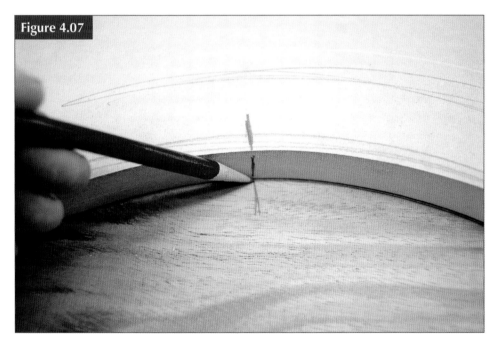

Figure 4.07.

Figure 4.06. Mark a parallel line (which represents the seam) ½" inside the template on the board. You can use dividers or a circular parallel drawing disc as a spacer to hold your pencil ½" away from the line.

Figure 4.07. Trace the edge of the OD template onto the board, too, and a registration line onto both parts for future realignment.

Figure 4.08. Remove the hardwood from the OD template and cut the blank about $1/16''$ inside this seam line with a band saw or jigsaw. Note: jigsaws often do not cut perpendicular when cutting curves, so perform a test and cut farther away from the line if necessary.

Figure 4.09–4.11. Realign and install the wood blank securely onto the OD template, screwing in the safe zone. Transfer the butt joint locations onto the board.

Figure 4.08

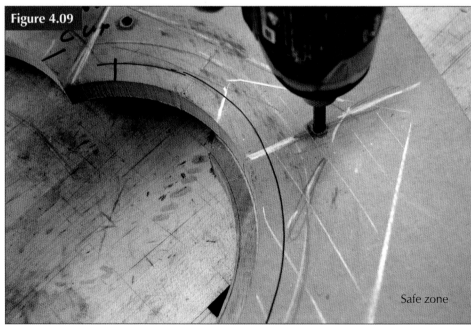

Figure 4.09

Safe zone

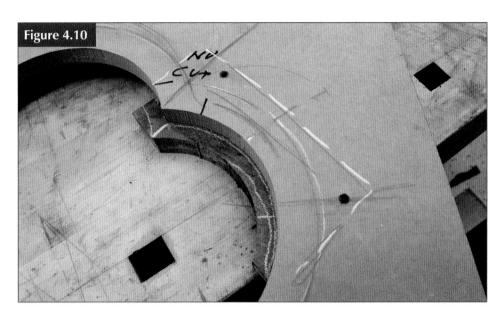

Figure 4.10

Figure 4.11

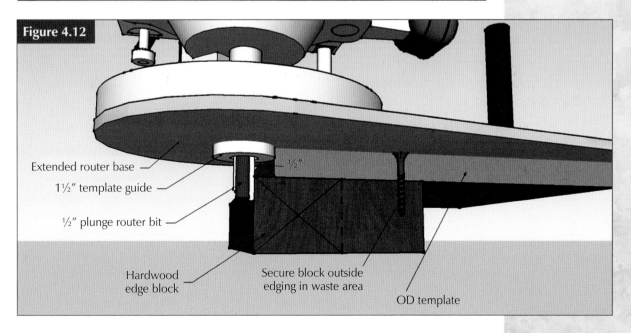

Figure 4.12

Extended router base

1½" template guide

½" plunge router bit

½"

Hardwood
edge block

Secure block outside
edging in waste area

OD template

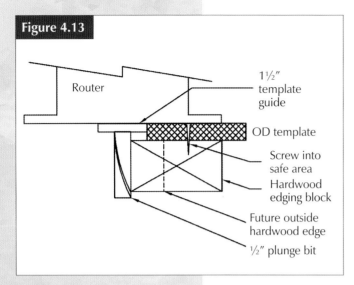

Figure 4.13

Router

1½" template guide

OD template

Screw into safe area

Hardwood edging block

Future outside hardwood edge

½" plunge bit

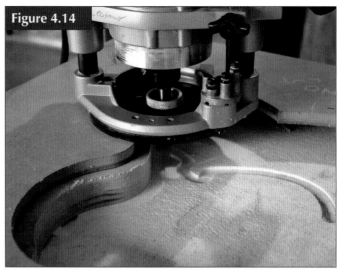

Figure 4.14

Figures 4.13–4.15. Securely clamp the entire assembly to a bench and router the inside edge with the custom 1½" template guide. A spoiler board can be used as shown in figure 4.14 to prevent cutting into your bench. Note: on tight curves where end grain may be exposed, it may be necessary to perform a climb cut. See page 47.

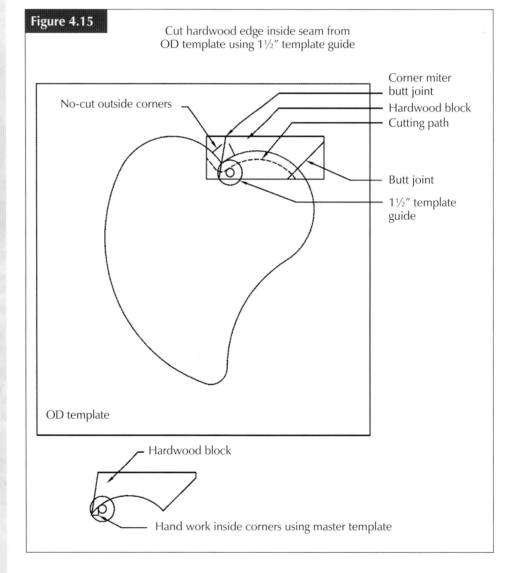

Figure 4.15

Cut hardwood edge inside seam from OD template using 1½" template guide

No-cut outside corners

Corner miter butt joint

Hardwood block

Cutting path

Butt joint

1½" template guide

OD template

Hardwood block

Hand work inside corners using master template

Preventing Tear-Out: Standard Cutting Direction Versus a Climb Cut

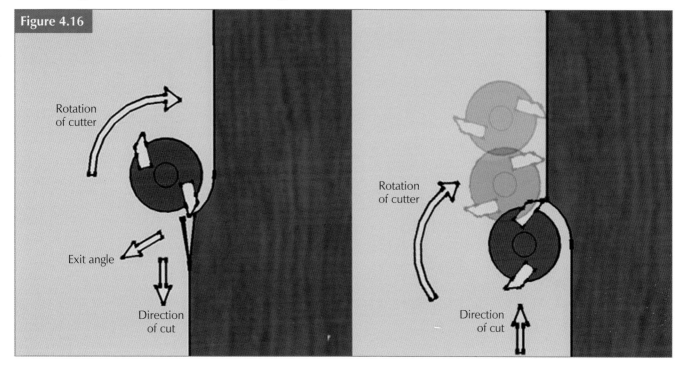

Figure 4.16

A router bit typically spins clockwise, and in a conventional cut you push the router against the direction of the spinning bit. In other words, the piece is fed against the rotation of the router bit, similar to using a circular saw or table saw. This is the safest method. The cutter exits outward, pulling material away and possibly chipping more wood than you intended, which is called tear-out. Multiple shallow passes can help minimize tear-out but don't always prevent it.

When tear-out is persistent, especially when encountering end grain, a climb cut is necessary. Climb cutting is when you move the router in the direction of the bit rotation. Think of it as a spinning wheel that you move in the same direction.

If you do not hold the router firmly, the bit can climb up and run along the wood. This is dangerous and happens in a split second. That said, the advantage of this cut is that the cutter enters the wood at the point of contact and compresses the wood inward, preventing tear-out. Be very careful when doing this type of cut.

In lieu of a double-fluted straight bit, a spiral router bit can also minimize tear-out. With a spiral bit, the actual cutting blade twists around the bit, which cuts at a slight angle. Bits can spiral up, down, or both up and down (called a compression bit). These bits are typically solid carbide and pricey, but well worth the investment. See fig. 4.17 on page 48.

Straight, Spiral, and Compression Router Bits

Figure 4.17

Figure 4.17. Up-and-down spiral bits are the most expensive and the best of both worlds. I use the spiral down bit or the up-and-down (compression) bit.

A spiral up bit helps hold the router base down to the cutting surface and cleans out the dust it creates from the kerf, but it can also tear out the top surface, especially on a pre-veneered top. Down spirals move the material downward and compress the top surface, but this makes the router a bit more unstable.

Figure 4.18

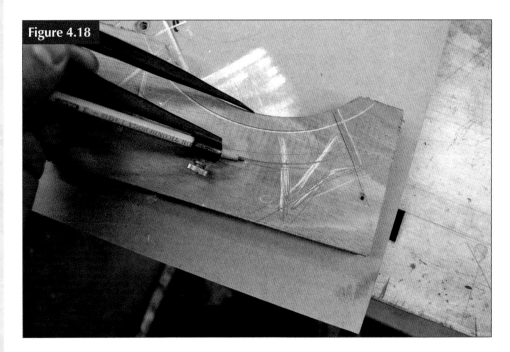

Figure 4.19

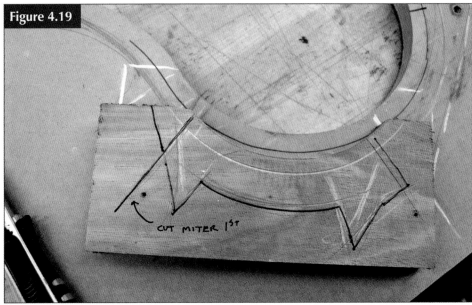

Figures 4.18–4.19. After routing the seam edge, remove it from the template and mark the perimeter edge, which is the width of the final edge. This may be parallel or tapered. If it tapers, sketch it in roughly and leave plenty of room for changes. It is always best to err on the thick side and cut more material off once the edge is glued onto the field. Also add clamping tabs on each end. These will help pull the end butt joints together during glue-up and clamping, so these tabs have to be flat and parallel to the butt joint. On very odd-shaped tables, additional clamping tabs may be needed to keep the clamps from sliding, depending on the direction of the clamps.

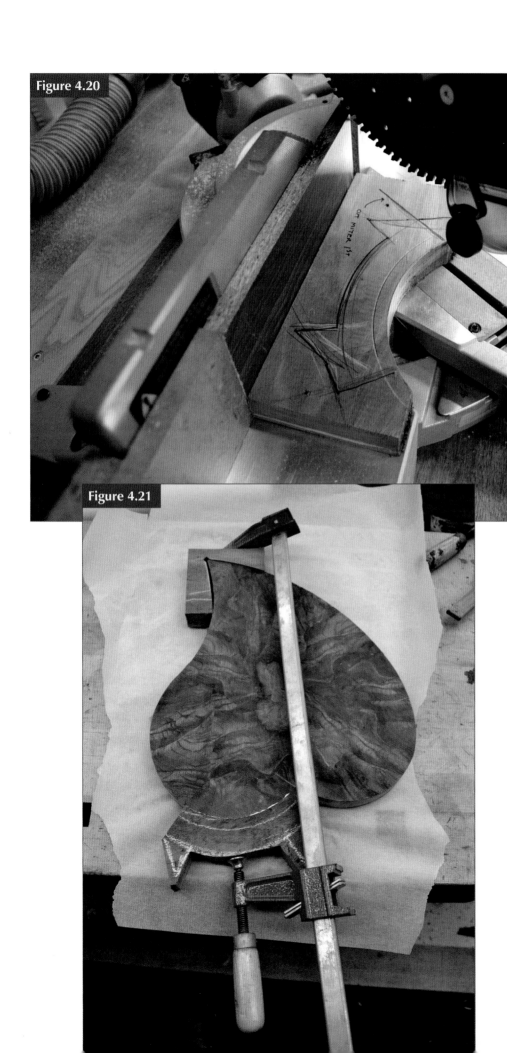

Figure 4.20.

Figure 4.21.

Figure 4.20. Cut the butt seams on both ends with a chop box (miter saw), using the outside straight edge of the hardwood against the fence. You can also do this on a band saw and clean up the cut with a disc sander. In both cases, be sure the cut is square vertically. Cut the outside edge on a band saw, just outside the drawn perimeter line, and remember to add clamping tabs on each end.

Figure 4.21. Align and glue this first piece on the field and leave the top hardwood surface of the edging proud (high) by 1/16" or so.

Figure 4.25. To avoid mashing the opposite field edge, you might also have to make special clamping blocks for the other side of the table and/or provide a flat surface for the clamp end

Figure 4.26. On larger tables and longer pieces, add biscuits or a spline to help with this alignment. Note: do not use biscuits if the tapered edge will be very thin, because the biscuits will poke through when the edging's outside face is cut.

Clamping Methods

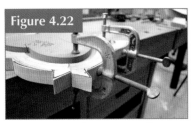

Figure 4.22. Three-way edge clamp.

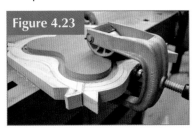

Figure 4.23. One-handed edge clamp that uses offset cams to pinch the table.

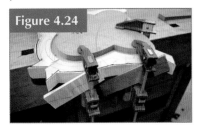

Figure 4.24. Clamps with wedges.

A number of clamping methods can be used; typically bar and pipe clamps do the trick. Be sure not to compress or damage the hardwood edge, or top or bottom of the field. Always use clamping blocks to protect these areas.

Figure 4.25

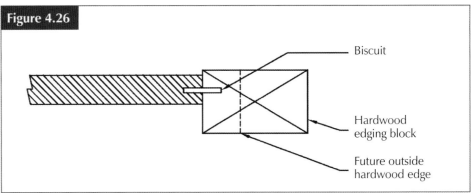

Figure 4.26

Biscuit

Hardwood edging block

Future outside hardwood edge

Once the first piece of edging is glued on, things can move along at a faster pace. For the next hardwood piece, repeat step 6 on either side of the first one.

Figure 4.27

Figure 4.27. To cut the mating butt joint perfectly, place the board blank under the field, align the seam cut to the field edge, and overlap it to the first butt joint. You can tilt the board slightly to catch, align, and rest it on the seam edge face and mark the joint.

Figure 4.28. Score the overlapped butt joint with a marking knife to scribe the joint precisely.

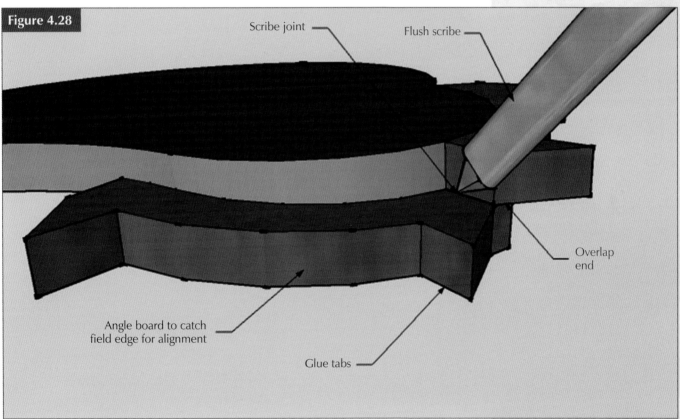

Figure 4.28

Scribe joint

Flush scribe

Overlap end

Angle board to catch field edge for alignment

Glue tabs

Figures 4.29–4.30. Cut the butt joint on a band saw slightly proud and fine tune on a disc sander.

Figure 4.31. Check the fit and be sure the butt joint is perfect.

Figure 4.29

Figure 4.30

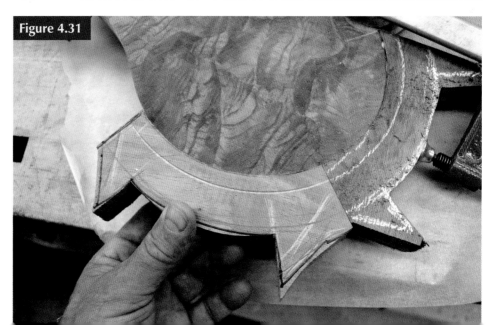

Figure 4.31

Note: It is important to fit the butt joint before cutting the outside perimeter. If your butt joint is too short, you can always screw it onto the OD template, shifting it inward a tad. Rerouting the seam will give you slightly more length on the butt joint so you can rework it for a perfect fit. Practice makes perfect.

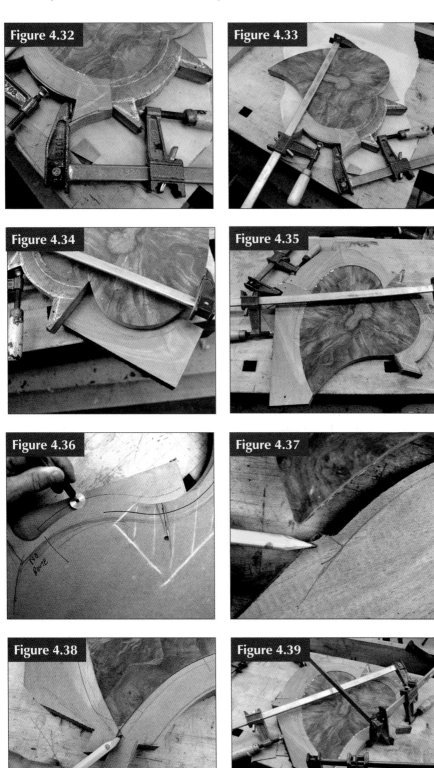

Figure 4.32

Figure 4.33

Figure 4.34

Figure 4.35

Figure 4.36

Figure 4.37

Figure 4.38

Figure 4.39

Figures 4.32–4.33. Clamp the edge on lightly at first and clamp the butt joints tightly to ensure they won't move. Then firm up all the other clamps and move on to the next piece on the other side.

Figures 4.34–4.35. Once the second piece is glued on, switch to the other side of the first piece, cut the third piece, fit it, and clamp it on.

Figures 4.36–4.37. For outside corners where the OD template has rounded corners, the seam edge on the hardwood cannot be completely routed to the end of the hardwood: this seam will have to be hand worked. The master template can help you extend the line and cut with a band saw, sawing close to the line and sanding for a perfect fit.

Figures 4.38–4.39. Fitting the last piece in is the most tedious because it has to fit perfectly on both ends. Work very slowly on this step, testing the fit with each adjustment. Once a tight match is achieved, glue into place. Sometimes the hardwood moves and cups a bit after the rough cut, so use a firm hand and clamp to snug the seam tight.

Figure 4.40. An offset router base can be made easily by using scrap plywood or MDF. With the ID template removed, the extended router base has an offset ¼" spacer to allow the router base and bit to float over the table field and cut the protruding hardwood edge flush to the field.

Flushing the Hardwood Edge

Once the edge glue has dried and the clamps are removed, the proud hardwood can be machined down flush to the veneer field top. This can be done with the ID template on or off.

There are a variety of reasons I might take off the ID template: the table design, the need for speed and accuracy, the risk of damaging the ID template or veneer top, the type of inlay, and so on.

If you leave the ID template on, use a router with an extended base and drop the bit down a skooch above the veneered field.

If you remove the ID template, use either a router with extended base and shim spacer (fig. 4.40) or a lipping planer. I like to use a lipping planer, which is much faster.

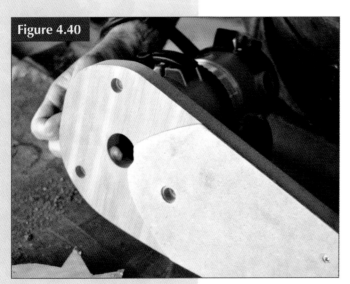
Figure 4.40

Figure 4.41

Figure 4.41. A lipping planer has the cutter head off to the side, while the body of the machine rests firmly on the table. These machines are pricey but fast and accurate.

Figure 4.42. On small tables, and if you have removed the ID template, an additional shim sheet might be needed to prevent the tail of the offset router base from hitting the protruding edge on the opposite side of the table. This shim sheet can be the ID template, although I don't like to risk hitting and damaging this template, so I rough-cut another one out of scrap. It doesn't matter how thick this piece is, as the router bit can be lowered to adjust for it.

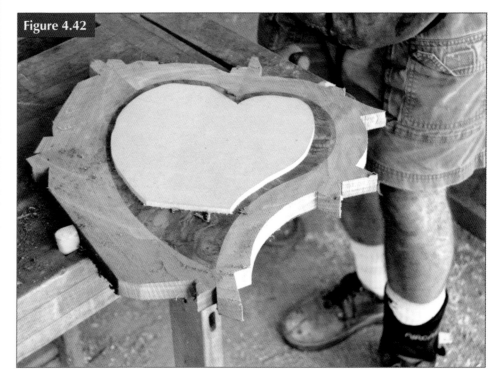
Figure 4.42

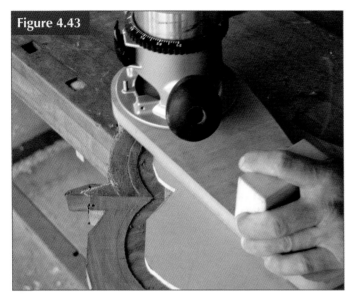

Figure 4.43

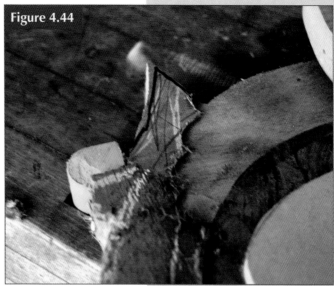

Figure 4.44

Figure 4.45

Figures 4.43–4.46. Example of flushing hardwood edge with ID template removed and a shim sheet added so the router base will clear and float over the proud hardwood edge. Set the bit so it barely kisses the veneer, and then raise it by a hair. Slowly router the edge flush and work your way around, holding the base steady.

Figure 4.46

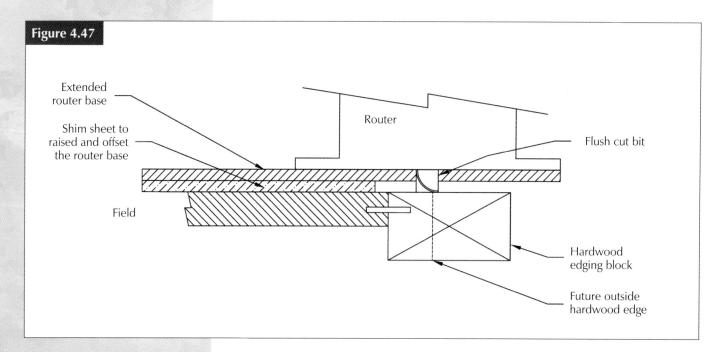

Figure 4.47

Extended router base

Shim sheet to raised and offset the router base

Router

Flush cut bit

Field

Hardwood edging block

Future outside hardwood edge

Figure 4.48. Repeat this flush trimming process for the back side. By adding a thicker shim sheet, the hardwood can be trimmed flush or you can leave a hardwood lip (or drop edge) that hangs down past the bottom of the field. The greater the drop edge, the thicker the shim sheet needs to be.

Figure 4.48

Figure 4.49

Figure 4.50

Figure 4.49–4.50. If you keep the ID template on, there is a risk of hitting it with the router bit, which can damage it and affect future steps. I've added two wooden dowel pins on the router base to keep the bit from hitting the template.

Step 7. Cutting the Outside Edge

The ID template allows you to cut the outside edge parallel with the seam. I will demonstrate both scenarios of cutting the outside edge in the following steps, as my heart table has both parallel and tapered edges.

If you removed the ID template, reinstalling it can be a challenge, especially with organic and odd-shaped forms. In this case, the ID template now needs to be re-adhered and centered on the field, leaving *exactly* ½" between the field and the seam on all sides.

Figure 4.51–4.52. To accomplish this placement, first measure ½" in from the seam. I use dividers to duplicate this measurement and work my way around the form, marking every 6" or so. I've used a thick white pencil under my fine mechanical pencil mark for easier viewing in these photos.

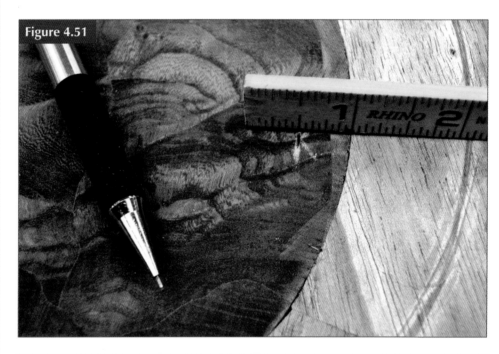

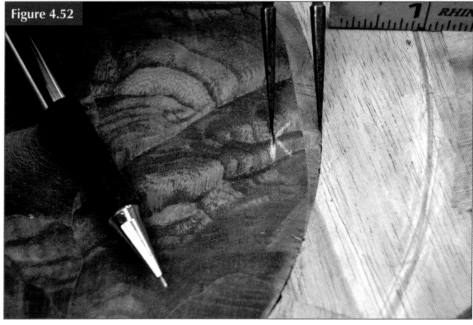

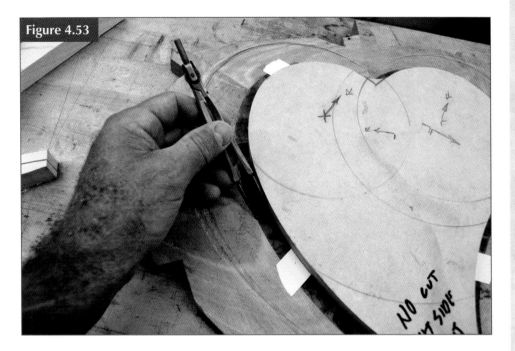

Figure 4.53.

Figure 4.54.

Figure 4.55.

Figure 4.53. Place the ID template on the field and shift it slightly back and forth until the distance is equal all around and aligned with the marks.

Figure 4.54. Hold the template firmly and use scrap blocks with double-stick tape to secure and register the template in place temporarily. Then remove the template, apply double-stick tape to the veneer field, and put it back within the registration blocks.

I like to use long securing blocks with double-stick on one end only. This allows me to move the long end left or right and twist to release the double-stick tape when it is time for removal.

Figure. 4.55. Sketch the outside edge where it is going to be tapered.

Figure 4.56

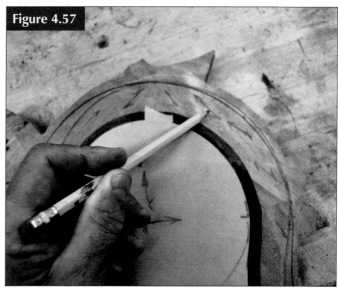

Figure 4.57

Figure 4.56. If all or a portion of the perimeter is parallel (the same edge width), identify these areas and draw a parallel 1½" line from the ID template. Again, this is for a 1" wide hardwood edge. You can use dividers or a spacer; I like to use a homemade large drawing disc 3" in diameter, which gives me a 1"-wide hardwood edge. To calculate the drawing disc diameter, the math goes like this: desired edge thickness of 1" plus the template offset of ½" equals 1½". Multiply that times two to get 3". See page 68 for instructions on how to make this and other diameter template bushings. See Making Template Guides, page 68, for instructions on how to make this and other diameter template bushings.

Figure 4.57. Mark the grain direction on the edge. This helps to determine where you may need to make a climb cut to prevent tear-out.

Figure 4.58–4.59. Rough-cut just outside the parallel line on the band saw. Don't cut the transitional tapered areas yet.

Figure 4.58

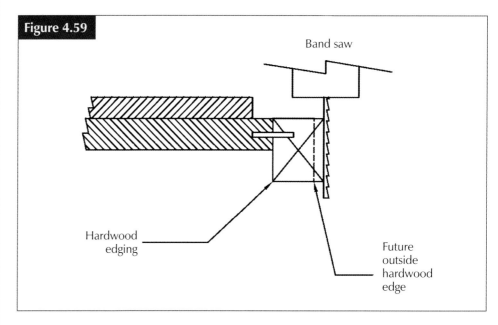

Figure 4.59

Band saw

Hardwood edging

Future outside hardwood edge

Figure 4.60

Figure 4.61

Figures 4.60–4.63. With a 3½″ template guide, router the outside edge. Note: there is minimal contact between the router base and the top of the original template, so an extended router base is required (fig. 4.65).

Figure 4.62

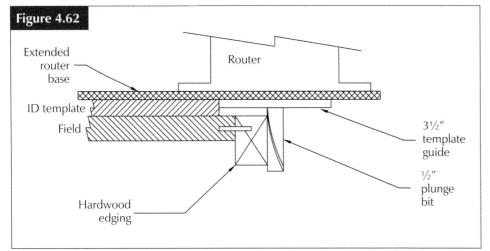

Extended router base

Router

ID template

Field

3½″ template guide

½″ plunge bit

Hardwood edging

Figure 4.63   Cut outside of hardwood with ID template using 3½″ template guide. Don't cut around outside corners.

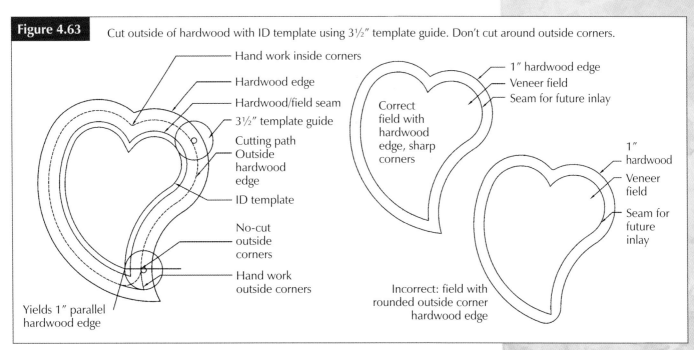

Hand work inside corners

Hardwood edge

Hardwood/field seam

3½″ template guide

Cutting path
Outside hardwood edge

ID template

No-cut outside corners

Hand work outside corners

Yields 1″ parallel hardwood edge

1″ hardwood edge
Veneer field
Seam for future inlay

Correct field with hardwood edge, sharp corners

1″ hardwood
Veneer field
Seam for future inlay

Incorrect: field with rounded outside corner hardwood edge

Figure 4.64

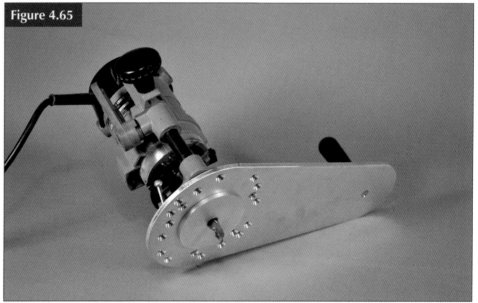

Figure 4.65

Use an extended offset router base with a 3½" template guide to router the outside hardwood edge. This is a risky operation—without an extended base, you have minimal surface area on the router base. **Do not attempt this**.

If you make your own template guide bushing as described on page 68, it can be made the same thickness as the ID template (typically ½"). This will also act as a steady rest. Finally, do not cut all the way through the hardwood in one step. This will strain the router and possibly chip the hardwood. I like to take off ¼" in each pass.

Remember to use a spoiler board (a sheet of material that the router can cut into) or leave a lip and flush-cut it once the perimeter has been shaped, as seen in previous steps.

Note where climb cuts are required and cut them slowly. Depending on the species and the hardness of the wood edging, a number of passes may be required. Use the plunge function on the router to cut ¼" on each pass.

Figure 4.66

Figure 4.67

Figure 4.66–4.67. Cut off the remaining transitional edging with a band saw or jigsaw.

Figures 4.68–4.71. Sand the outside edges and pay special attention to the transition of the curve. Feel the curves and remove any slight humps or bumps.

Figure 4.68

Figure 4.69

Figure 4.70

Figure 4.71

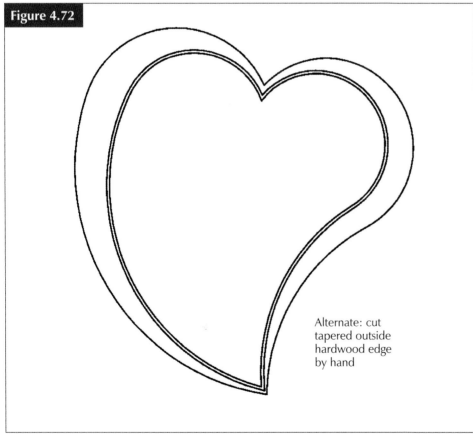

Figure 4.72

Alternate: cut
tapered outside
hardwood edge
by hand

Figure 4.72. Transitioning the
width of the hardwood edge
freehand on a band saw is
easy to do and adds more
expression to your work.

5.
Inlay

Step 8. Inlay

Any size of inlay groove can be accurately cut with this system, and any type of inlay can be installed—for example, a single wood strip, multiple strips, silver, mother-of-pearl, or colored epoxy, to name just a few.

Figure 5.01. Small gaps may occur in the seam between the hardwood edging and veneer field that have to be concealed with filler or a decorative inlay. This gap typically shows up on smaller tables with tighter curved edges, and the hardwood won't flex during clamping. It is often due to unsteady machining or the slope in the template guide and router base.

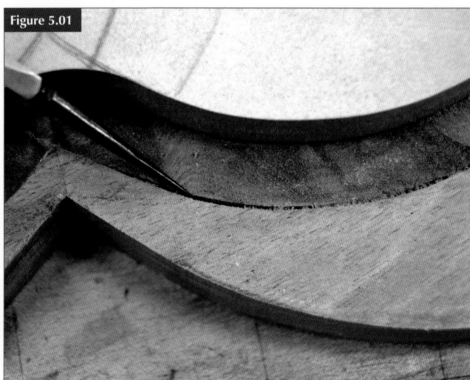

Figure 5.01

On larger, more graceful curves, the wood edging has much more flex and will typically set tight when clamped, so an inlay to hide this seam gap is unnecessary. However, an inlay can be a nice accent to your design.

The first and most important step is cutting the inlay groove dead center in the seam. For this you will need a 1″ template guide. In this case, the seam is the reference center line to the router bit. Because our ID template is ½″ from the seam, we double it to determine the guide diameter, giving us a center line to the router bit. Hence, a 1″ template guide is used.

Figure 5.02. Here I have made my own 1″ template guide out of wood turned on a lathe and glued onto a ⅝″ ID template guide. Stock 1″ template guides are available from most woodworking suppliers.

Figure 5.02

There are two ways to insert a wood veneer inlay: flat or vertical.

After the wood inlay is glued in and flushed to the tabletop, it sometimes develops fine tear-outs that need to be repaired with wood filler. Tape off the inlay to avoid smearing wood filler into the surrounding grain of the field or hardwood edge. This can be done before or after you router the groove.

Applying tape before you rout the groove is a great trick: use either masking tape or veneer tape. After you make the cut, the remaining tape is already aligned perfectly with the edge of the groove. This allows you to apply wood filler without getting it on the hardwood edge or veneer field (fig. 5.65 on page 88).

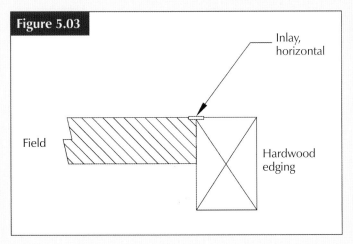

Figure 5.03

Inlay, horizontal

Field

Hardwood edging

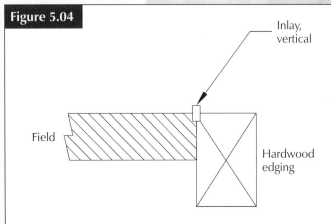

Figure 5.04

Inlay, vertical

Field

Hardwood edging

Making Template Guides

Figure 5.05

Figure 5.06

Figure 5.07

To make your own template guide and scribe disc, a simple jig on the disc sander will yield quick and accurate results. This jig also allows for minor adjustments and fine tuning for odd situations that may come up.

In this example I use a standard, store-bought $^5/_{16}$" OD template guide. Using a $^5/_{16}$" drill bit, drill a ¼" piece of MDF and cut it roughly larger than the final outer diameter of the new 1" bushing. Install the drill bit upside down, a little less than ½" centered from the edge of the jig bed (¾" MDF).

With a fence clamped on the bottom of the jig and aligned with the disc sander bed, push the jig into the disc, rotate the new MDF bushing, and

create a perfect circular disc centered with the template guide hole. Is this description clear as mud? Look at figure 5.06.

I like to coat my newly made bushing with CA glue (CA = cyanoacrylate, or Super Glue®) to give it a little more hardness and stability. You can also add a pivoting feature to the jig for finer adjustments.

Using MDF in the same thickness as your ID template stabilizes the router, which acts as a steady rest and eliminates the possibility of tipping during the final outside edge trimming. This technique can be used to make larger guides including the 3½" diameter bushing shown previously.

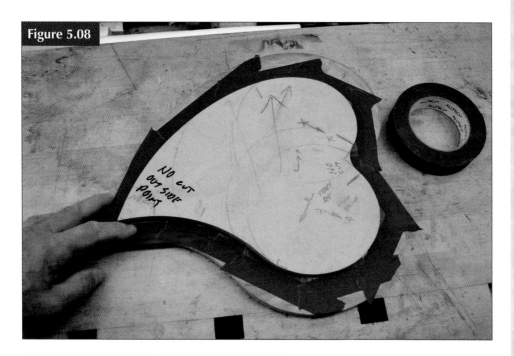

Figure 5.08

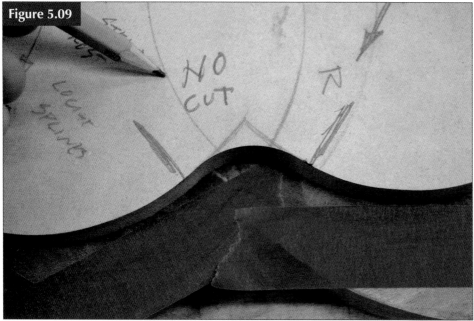

Figure 5.09

Figure 5.10

Figures 5.08–5.10. If installing the inlay flat (horizontal), then cut the groove just shy of the inlay veneer thickness. To do this, put a layer of masking tape over the seam and register the router bit to it, minus the inlay thickness, which leaves the veneer slightly high when installed. It is just proud enough to be sanded perfectly flush later. Remember to note the no-cut outside corners. Have I said that enough?

Figure 5.11

Figure 5.11. To adjust the depth of the groove, lower the plunge router bit so it just kisses the tape, then lower the depth gauge on the router and use a piece of the inlay as a gauge. When the veneer is removed from the router gauge, you can lower the bit to the exact thickness of the inlay.

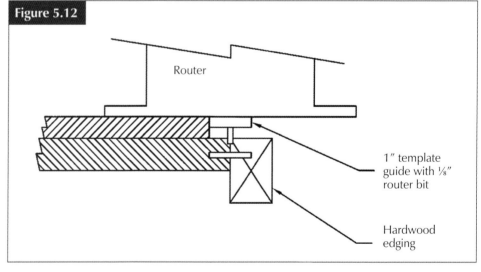

Figure 5.12

Router

1" template guide with ⅛" router bit

Hardwood edging

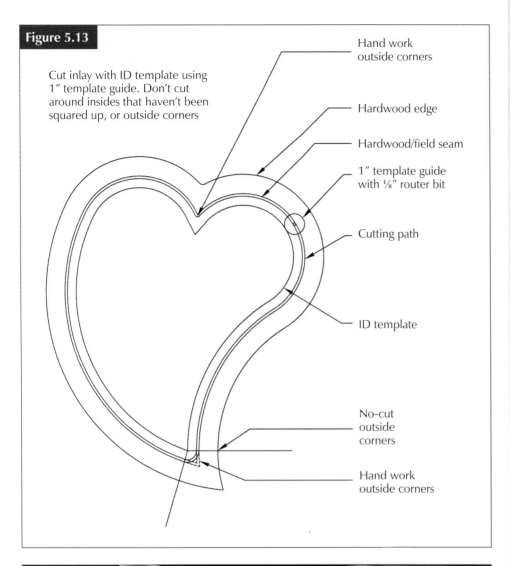

Figure 5.13

Cut inlay with ID template using 1" template guide. Don't cut around insides that haven't been squared up, or outside corners

Hand work outside corners

Hardwood edge

Hardwood/field seam

1" template guide with ⅛" router bit

Cutting path

ID template

No-cut outside corners

Hand work outside corners

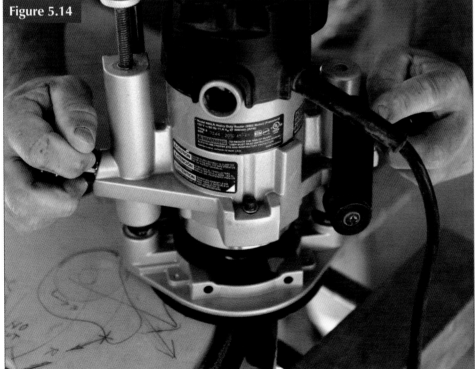

Figure 5.14

Figure 5.14. Router the groove with a single pass and remember to avoid the no-cut areas on outside corners.

Figure 5.15. Remember not to router around the no-cut corners. Have I said that enough?

Figure 5.15

Figure 5.16

For this project, I laminated five strips of contrasting veneer and installed them vertically on edge, removing the blue tape for better visibility. Typically a vertical inlay is left higher than a horizontally installed one and needs to be machined flush instead of just sanded, so veneer tape works best here (see fig. 5.63 on page 88).

Figure 5.17

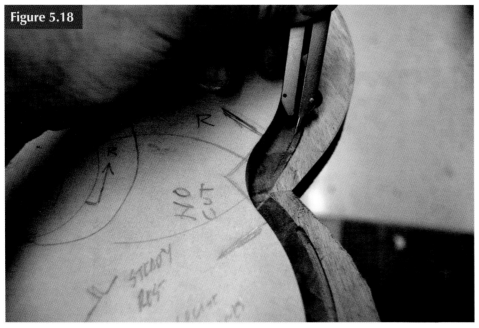

Figure 5.18

Figure 5.17–5.18. Whichever way you chose to install the inlay, the no-cut areas need to be cut by hand; various methods and techniques work. With the ID template in place, I use it as a guide to score each side of the groove lines parallel to the template. In this example, I use a knife installed in my dividers and score each side of the groove as far as I can before the template curves in the corner. You can also glue razor blades to shims for this operation.

Figure 5.19

Figure 5.19. Now it is time to remove the ID template from the field. A sharp chisel and slight downward pressure typically does the trick. Do not lift the handle end of the chisel, as this will gouge the veneer field. For stubborn pieces, squirt a little mineral spirits or paint thinner solvent to loosen the double-stick adhesive. Work slowly.

Figure 5.20. With the template removed, use it as guide or use the duplicate master pattern for hand cutting each side of the groove.

Figures 5.21–5.23. Once each side of the groove is scored, chisel it out. This can be done with a utility knife, surgical scalpel, or fine chisel. I use a custom micro chisel made from an old dental pick. Sharpen to the exact width of the groove and chisel out the remaining material. Grinding an old hacksaw blade made of hardened steel works well, too. Inside corners have to be squared up, as they will have a 1/16" radius left from the router bit.

Figure 5.20

Figure 5.21

Figure 5.22

Figure 5.23

Figure 5.24

Figure 5.24. Clean up the entire groove with fine sandpaper (180 grit) and you are ready to go.

Inlay Veneer

A number of specialty manufacturers offer stock veneer inlay strips in a variety of widths, species, and patterns. Search under wood inlay or "luthier purfling" for suppliers. Some companies will custom cut to your specifications; these inlays are laser cut and very accurate. They have to be installed horizontally flat and a tight radius can be a challenge, if not impossible. Some suppliers offer radius curved pieces, too.

Figure 5.25. Stock inlays come in a variety of complex patterns. *Inlay courtesy of Dover Designs*

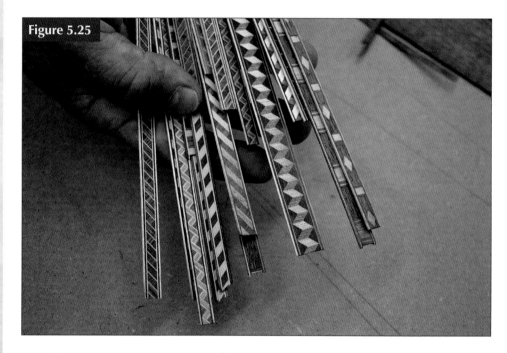

Figure 5.25

Making Your Own—Hand Cutting

Making your own inlay is an easy way to go, and you can use a variety of methods to slice it.

If the veneer is to be inlaid flat/horizontal, you must cut the veneer precisely. The strip needs to be parallel, with a consistent width from strip to strip. Typically a project will require a number of strips to inlay the complete perimeter of the table. To cut these strips, purchase a handheld slicer and use a straight edge.

Figure 5.26. With a homemade slicer (left), design courtesy of Michael Fortune, or a commercially bought one (as seen on the right), single sheets can be easily cut into inlay strips.

Figure 5.26

Figure 5.27

Figure 5.27. First, measure the distance from the blade to the slicer edge (in this case 2.3 mm on my commercial slicer), then add the width of the desired inlay (3 mm). Adding these values together equals 5.3 mm for the offset spacer. My spacer is made from two offset layers of ⅛″ poplar double-stick-taped together. It is best to make one and then cut it in half to ensure the spacers are exactly alike.

Slide the veneer under your straight edge and, using the spacers, set the 5.3 mm distance from the edge of the veneer to the face of the straight edge. I like to add small strips of 100-grit PSA sandpaper on the bottom of the straight edge to prevent it from sliding while cutting. Make your cut with the slicer and voila! 3 mm inlay veneer.

Figure 5.28

Figures 5.28–5.29. A variety of slicers are commercially available; each works a little differently, but all yield good results for onesy-twosy cuts.

Figure 5.29

Making Your Own—Using a Jig

For cutting multiple strips, I like to use a table saw sled jig. This will accurately cut multiple pieces at a time.

Figures 5.30–5.31. Set the adjustable jig fence to ⅛" (3 mm) width, which is the width of the inlay you want to make. *Photo courtesy of Marc Adams School of Woodworking, jig made by Mark Hedin*

Figure 5.30

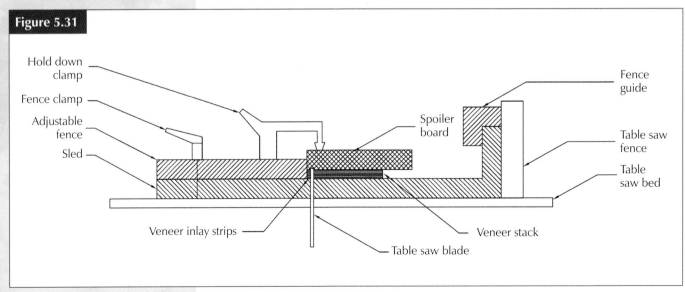

Figure 5.31

Hold down clamp

Fence clamp

Adjustable fence

Sled

Spoiler board

Fence guide

Table saw fence

Table saw bed

Veneer inlay strips

Table saw blade

Veneer stack

Figure 5.32

Figure 5.33

Figure 5.34

Figures 5.32–5.34. Place the stack of veneer tightly against the jig fence. Place a waste spoiler board on top and use toggle clamps to hold the veneer firmly in place during cutting.

Figure 5.35. Hold the sled against the table saw fence with a temporary interlocking plywood guide to ensure a consistent, equal, and straight cut. This also prevents it from tilting off the table saw while pulled back, and you can load more veneer while the saw is still running.

Figure 5.36. You can cut multiple strips of different species in exactly the same width. Repeat cuts can be set up, then sliced quickly. This system can also be used for thicker veneer or thin hardwood.

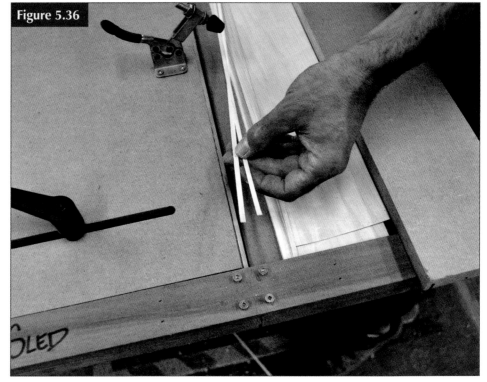

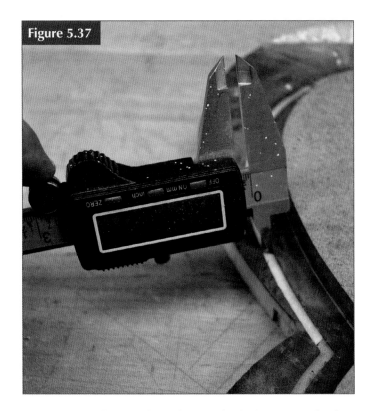

Figure 5.37

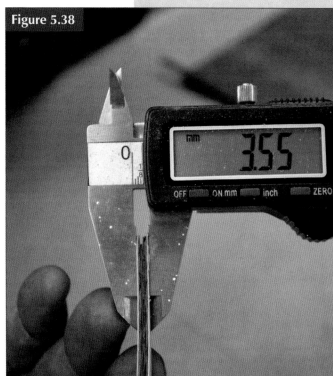

Figure 5.38

For vertical, on-edge inlay, multiple layers are built up, either in the same species to create a solid color or in a combination of contrasting species to create a fine pin stripe or stringing inlay. In either case, the stack of veneer will need to be slightly thinner than the inlay groove. Be sure that the veneer slides easily in and out of the groove, because during gluing, the veneer will swell to a tight fit. In many cases, a few strips of inlay need to be thinned down.

A thickness veneer scraper jig is simple to make. Clamp a scraper at 55 degrees securely against a smooth, hard surface. Slide the veneer under the scraper, slide the scraper down to rest on it, and lightly tighten the clamps. Remove the veneer and tap the scraper lightly to move it down ever so slightly and tighten the clamps.

Hand sand the end of the inlay strip so it is thin enough to fit under the scraper or with a pivoting option on the jig (see figs. 5.39–5.40 on page 82), rotate the scraper up, and slide the inlay under. With pliers, pull the veneer through the scraper, scraping it to an even thickness. Repeat if a thinner dimension is desired.

Figures 5.37–5.38. Measure the groove width and check it against a stack of veneer. It is a good idea to make it slightly thinner to allow for swelling when the glue is applied.

Figures 5.39–5.40. If the stack of veneer is too thick or a thinner layer is desired for an aesthetic reason, a layer of veneer can be scraped down by hand or by using a thickness scraping jig. *Design courtesy of Michael Fortune and the Marc Adams School of Woodworking*

Figure 5.41. A handheld version of this thickness scraper can be purchased or made with tooling steel from an old band saw or hacksaw blade. These are permanently set with wide gaps; use your finger to apply pressure to the inlay and the scraper edge while pulling.

Figure 5.39

Figure 5.40

Figure 5.41

There are various techniques for installing multiple layers of veneer inlay, based on the flexibility of the veneer, the tightness of the curve, and the number of layers being installed. Some veneer can be unruly; it can chip or break during installation and require pre-bending. In some cases, gluing the layers together makes installation easier.

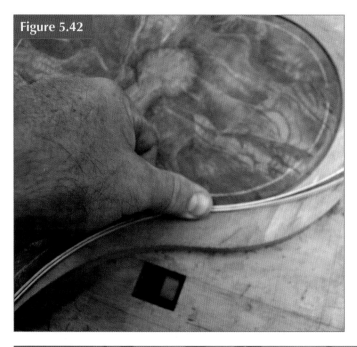

Figure 5.42

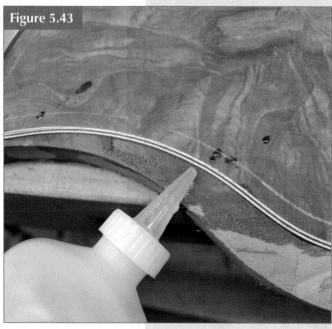

Figure 5.43

Figure 5.44

Figure 5.45

Figure 5.42. Test the fit of stacked inlay to be sure it has a snug, but not tight, fit.

Figure 5.43. If the test fit slides in cleanly, it can be glued in place with CA glue, which has a low viscosity and will penetrate all the layers and seams. Or you can use a fine bead of white glue in the groove before installing the inlay (not shown).

Figures 5.44–5.45. With tighter curves, the layers may need to be glued together and pre-bent. Use the master pattern as a form and cover the edge with cellophane tape to prevent glue from sticking to it. Coat the inlay layers lightly with PVA glue and tape securely to the ID template. Perform a glue test on a small section to see if the wood swells too much to fit into the inlay groove. Additional scraping may be necessary.

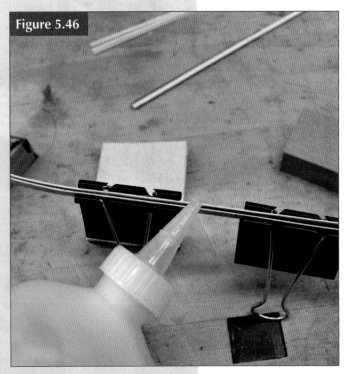

Figure 5.46

Figure 5.47

Figure 5.46. Another method for straight sections or gentle curves is to use paper clips and CA glue to tack the layers together. This is a good technique for longer runs and will help keep all the strips together. Note: CA glue is not flexible, so once the layers are glued together they will not bend.

Figure 5.47. Another way to create tight bends is to heat the inlay with an iron and spritz with a little water.

Figures 5.48–5.49. If the corners have very tight radii, use veneer softener to create tight bends. Commercial softeners are available, or you can make a home brew with three parts water, two parts PVA glue, one part glycerin, and one part alcohol. Soak the inlay in the mixture for a few minutes, and it will bend into the tightest curves.

Figure 5.48

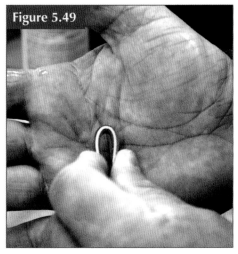

Figure 5.49

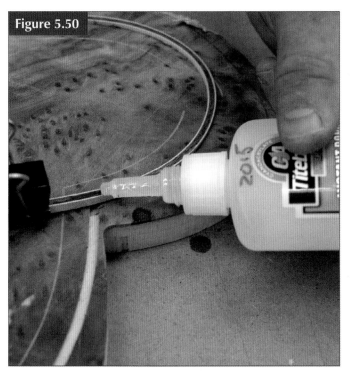

Figure 5.50

Figure 5.51

Figure 5.52

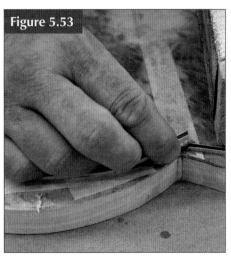

Figure 5.53

Figures 5.50–5.55. Fitting the seams and corner joints together can be quite tedious. Use a magnifying glass or a jeweler's visor so you can see what is going on. Each layer can be hand cut one at a time; I prefer pre-gluing layers at the ends so I can work the stack together. I use a protective sheet under the inlay while I cut the joint with a sharp chisel, and then touch up the joint with a sanding block. This is micro joinery at its best.

Figure 5.54

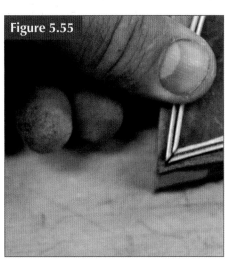

Figure 5.55

Figure 5.56. After everything is fitted, install the inlay securely. On occasion, a little light tapping with a hammer and block of wood (for even pressure) is required to coerce the pieces into the groove to seat the inlay tight to the bottom.

Figure 5.57. If the inlay was installed horizontally and flat, only light scraping and/or sanding is required to flush it up to the veneered field and hardwood edge.

Figure 5.56

Figure 5.57

After the inlay glue is dry, it should be proud, sticking slightly above the table surface.

If the inlay was installed vertically and on edge, it will likely have more material sticking above the surface. Do not use a sander to remove this excess.

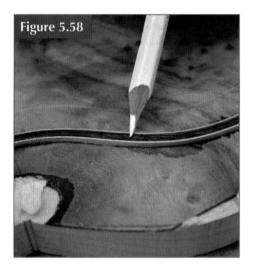

Figure 5.58

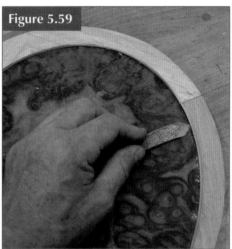

Figure 5.59

Figure 5.60

Figure 5.61

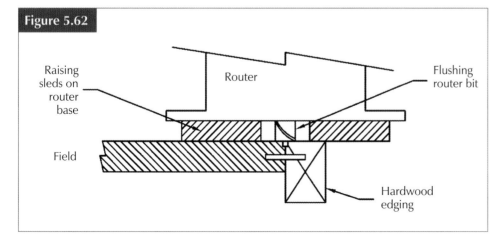

Figure 5.62

Raising sleds on router base

Router

Flushing router bit

Field

Hardwood edging

Figures 5.58–5.59. To remove this material, use a very sharp flush-cut marking scribe or chisel. Take your time—we do not want to tear out any of the inlay below the surface. Make multiple cuts with light passes.

Figures 5.60–5.62. Another method is to set up a small router with a flat-bottom bit and add two sled blocks on either side of the bit. This will allow the router base to clear the raised inlay so the bit can machine it flush. Or you can reinstall the ID template or shim sheet and use an offset router base. Either way, be sure not to go too deep and damage the thin veneer on the field.

Figure 5.63. If you forgot to install tape before routing the groove, no worries, simply tape over the groove and cut the opening with an Xacto® knife, using the groove as a guide (here I'm using veneer tape—my preference). You can add the tape after the inlay is installed, too, as shown in fig. 5.64. Masking tape will flex to accommodate the curves

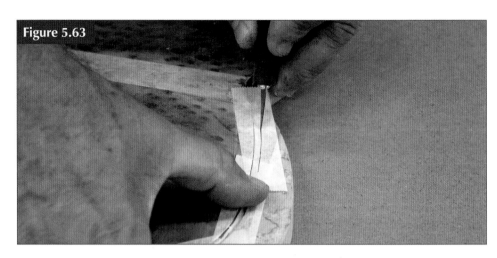

Figure 5.63

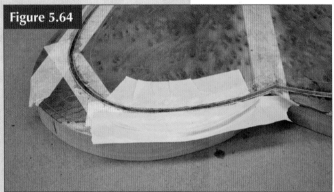

Figure 5.64

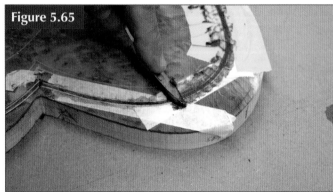

Figure 5.65

Figures 5.64–5.65. After the wood inlay is glued in and flushed close to the table top, it sometimes has fine tear-outs that need to be filled with wood filler. I typically use wood filler that matches the darkest inlay. Make sure you test the dry filler with finish to be sure you have a good match and fill the entire inlay over the tape. Don't just fill what you think is a hole, fill it all. After the filler is dry, remove the tape and sand the inlay flush.

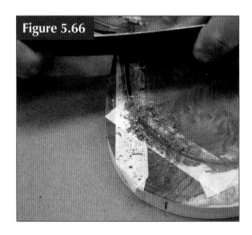

Figure 5.66

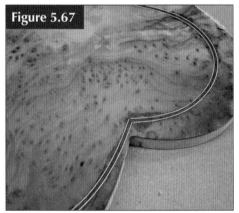

Figure 5.67

Figures 5.66–5.67. Hand scrape and/or sand the filler flush to the table to yield a perfect inlay detail.

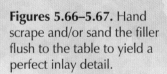

Figure 5.68

Congratulations! You now know how to apply a hardwood edge and inlay to any table shape.

With this system, hardwood edges can be applied easily, accurately, and quickly, whether it's an elegant French curved oval in a demilune table or a wild serpentine edge on a fun, artsy piece. Either way, I hope it opens up possibilities in your furniture designs.

Please consider reading my *Advanced Veneering and Alternative Techniques* book (Schiffer Publishing) to enhance your veneering skills, and visit my website, imaginegrove.com, to purchase some of the custom fixtures used in this book. Enjoy!

6. Tools

Below is a list of the tools I've used in step order. Not all are necessary, but you can certainly use this book as an excuse to buy a new tool.

- Soft lead pencil #2
- White pencil or chalk
- Tracing paper
- Masking tape: 1″ wide, low adhesion—blue, green, or yellow
- Compass
- Symmetrical drawing bow or thin strip of bending material like acrylic, Masonite, hardwood
- Asymmetrical drawing bow, tapered for French curves
- Band saw or jigsaw
- Disc sander, edge sander, or belt sander
- Spindle sander
- Sand paper, 80 grit
- Spoke shave
- File: coarse
- 1½″ HP plunge router
- ⅝″ OD template guide for router with custom-made 1½″ bushing. Available at scottgrove.com.
- ½″ rabbeting router bit, ½″ shank
- Router table
- Extended offset router base, store bought or homemade. Available at scottgrove.com.
- ½″ flush trim bit with ½″ shank for router (bottom bearing preferred)
- ½″ router bit with ½″ shank, prefer compression bit
- 1″ router bit
- Dividers
- Stick ruler
- Clamps: C, or adjustable for holding core in place
- Bar clamps: long adjustable, or edge clamps for clamping edging

- Double-stick tape or hot melt glue
- Automotive repair putty
- Screw gun and screws (1¼″)
- ½″ parallel drawing disc
- Chop box (miter saw)
- Biscuit cutter
- Utility knife, Xacto knife or surgical knife, flush scoring knife
- White or yellow PVA glue
- 3″ parallel drawing disc
- 3½″ custom-made template guide bushing
- 1″ template guide for router
- ⅛″ diameter router bit (or desired width for inlay)
- Sharp chisel, about 1″
- Dentist pick sharpened into narrow chisel for cleaning out inlay groove
- Inlay and/or tool to cut strips of inlay (various available or use a table saw jig)
- Veneer thickener for veneer inlay
- Scraper
- CA glue
- Iron for bending veneer
- Veneer softening solution: 3 parts water, 2 parts PVA glue,1 part glycerin, 1 part alcohol
- Magnifying glasses for inlay joinery
- Hammer
- Random orbital sander, various grits of sandpaper—120, 180, 220 grit
- Trim router with bottom flushing bit

Glossary

Drop edge: a table lip or downward overhang of a hardwood edge.

Biscuit: a flat, football-shaped piece of compressed wood used to join two pieces of wood together.

Edging or hardwood edge: material applied to the outside edge of the table. Softwood can also be used, but hardwood is more durable for table edging.

Hardwood edging block: the board that the curved hardwood edging is cut from.

ID (interior dimension) template: this template is precisely ½" smaller on all sides than the original table field.

Inlay: typically a thin strip of solid hardwood or thin wood veneer set into the tabletop, most often over the hardwood and table field seam. It can also be plastic, stone, or shell; a soft, metal-like silver or copper; or it can be a cured poured pigmented liquid like epoxy, urethane, or polyester.

Kerf: the void, groove, or gap that a cutter or saw blade makes.

Master pattern: table shape without the hardwood edging. It is a disposable pattern typically made from the ½" MDF that all templates are made from.

MDF: Medium-density fiberboard. This plywood-like material comes in a variety of thicknesses. It is very stable and consistent in thickness and composition.

OD (outside dimension) template: This template is used to cut the inside edge of the hardwood edging and is ½" larger than the table field.

Perimeter edge: the outside of the table hardwood edging.

Router: If you don't know what this tool is, or how to use it, give this book away or take a course in its proper use. A router spins a cutting tool called a router bit at high speed, typically between 6,000 and 10,000 rpms. I recommend using a minimum 1½" HP plunge router. A plunge router allows you to lower the router bit in a controlled manner.

Seam: the joint between the field and hardwood edge, typically covered by the inlay.

Shim sheet: a spacer made from sheet materials such as MDF, chipboard, or plywood.

Spoiler board: a waste sheet typically made from MDF, chipboard, EPS foam, or homasote that protects the workbench surface below the router blade.

Steady rest: a spacer used to prevent a router from tipping.

Stringing (inlay): thin veneer inlay, typically thin strips of veneer installed vertically or on edge.

Table field or field: tabletop to which the hardwood edging is applied; it is the same size as the original table pattern.

Tear-out: material that chips beyond the desired cutting line during machining.

Template guide: cylinder-shaped accessories that attach to a router base, allowing the router bit to protrude through them and keep the router bit a specific distance from a template during routing. It comes in a variety of sizes and is specified with inner and outer dimensions. Since most of the cutting is done with a ½" router bit, the ID of a template guide will need to be larger than ½", typically $\frac{17}{32}$" with a $\frac{5}{8}$" OD.

Template guide bushing: this custom-made bushing is doughnut-shaped, like a thick washer, and fits over a stock template guide. I refer to this combination as the template guide. A 1½" OD template guide is not available in stores. You can make your own or purchase one at imaginegrove.com.

Appendix: Steps 1–8 Condensed and Expanded

The following is a condensed list of the steps described in this book, followed by an expanded list and drawings for quick reference. Once you understand the fundamental principles, you can skip or combine some of them to save time and effort.

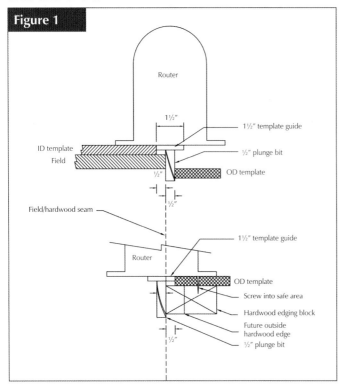

Figure 1

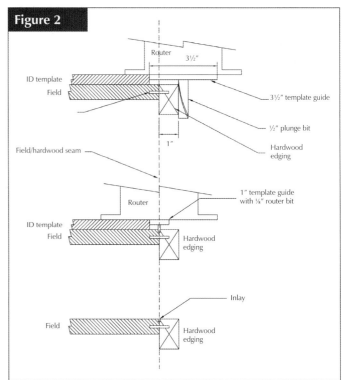

Figure 2

Steps: Condensed (Figures 1–2)

1. Master Pattern

2. Duplicate Master Pattern

3. ID Template

4. Field

5. OD template

6. Hardwood edge inside seam

7. Hardwood outside edge

8. Inlay

Steps: Expanded (Figures 3–18)

1. Master pattern

2. Duplicate master pattern

3. ID template
Reduce master pattern with ½" rabbet bit
Remove/flush rabbet lip

4. Field
Cut field
Rough saw rabbet lip
Remove rabbet lip, flush with router
Hand work corners

5. OD template
Rabbet cut
Drill and rough cut
Flush cut lip

6. Hardwood edge pattern inside seam
Rough cut inside edge
Fit cut inside edge
Cut end joints
Rough cut outside edge with gluing tabs
Glue on edging
Repeat—entire table edging
Flush hardwood top
Flush or drop-edge hardwood bottom

7. Hardwood outside edge
Rough cut
Final cut outside edge

8. Inlay
Route inlay groove
Install inlay
Flush inlay
Fill inlay
Scrape and sand final

Step 1. Master Pattern

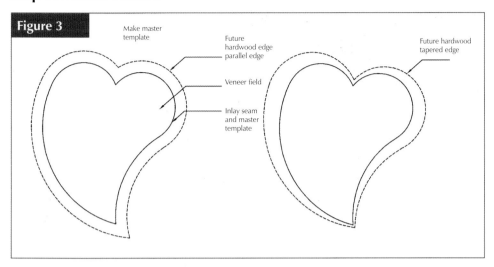

Figure 3

Make master template

Future hardwood edge parallel edge

Future hardwood tapered edge

Veneer field

Inlay seam and master template

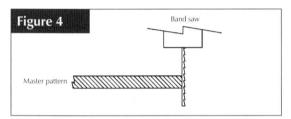

Figure 4

Band saw

Master pattern

Step 2. Duplicate Master Pattern

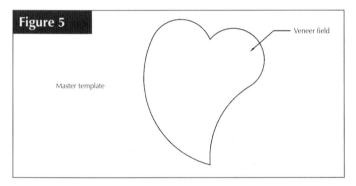

Figure 5

Master template

Veneer field

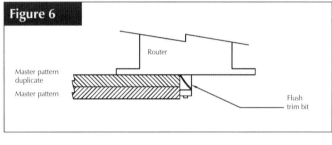

Figure 6

Router

Master pattern duplicate

Master pattern

Flush trim bit

Step 3. ID Template

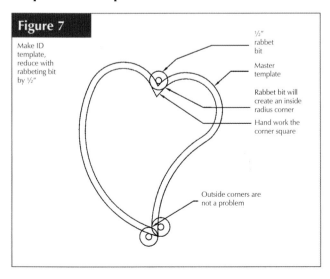

Figure 7

Make ID template, reduce with rabbeting bit by ½"

½" rabbet bit

Master template

Rabbet bit will create an inside radius corner

Hand work the corner square

Outside corners are not a problem

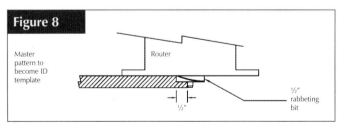

Figure 8

Master pattern to become ID template

Router

½" rabbeting bit

½"

Step 4. Field

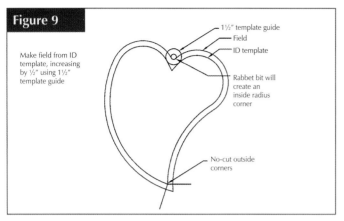

Figure 9

Make field from ID template, increasing by ½" using 1½" template guide

1½" template guide
Field
ID template

Rabbet bit will create an inside radius corner

No-cut outside corners

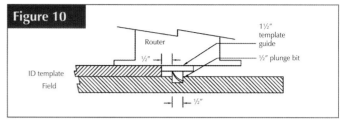

Figure 10

Router

½"

1½" template guide

½" plunge bit

ID template
Field

½"

Step 5. OD Template

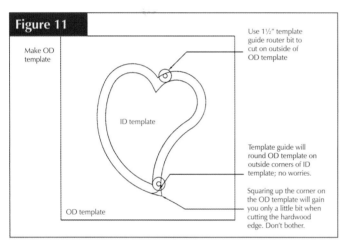

Figure 11

Make OD template

ID template

OD template

Use 1½" template guide router bit to cut on outside of OD template

Template guide will round OD template on outside corners of ID template; no worries.

Squaring up the corner on the OD template will gain you only a little bit when cutting the hardwood edge. Don't bother.

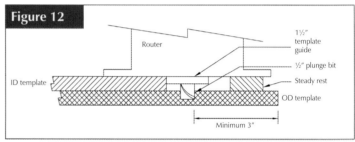

Figure 12

Router

1½" template guide

½" plunge bit

Steady rest

OD template

ID template

Minimum 3"

Step 6. Hardwood Seam

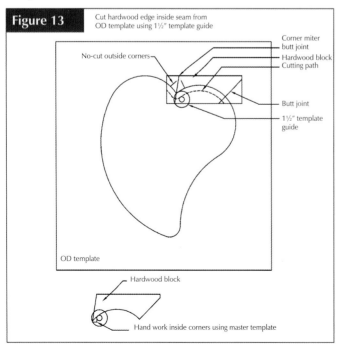

Figure 13

Cut hardwood edge inside seam from OD template using 1½" template guide

No-cut outside corners

Corner miter butt joint
Hardwood block
Cutting path

Butt joint

1½" template guide

OD template

Hardwood block

Hand work inside corners using master template

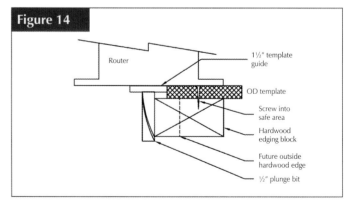

Figure 14

Router

1½" template guide

OD template

Screw into safe area

Hardwood edging block

Future outside hardwood edge

½" plunge bit

Step 7. Hardwood Outside Edge

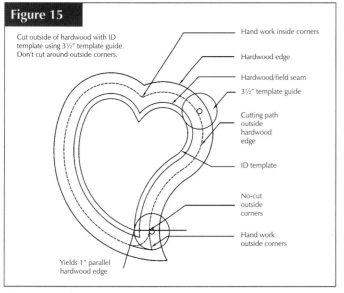

Figure 15

Cut outside of hardwood with ID template using 3½" template guide. Don't cut around outside corners.

- Hand work inside corners
- Hardwood edge
- Hardwood/field seam
- 3½" template guide
- Cutting path outside hardwood edge
- ID template
- No-cut outside corners
- Hand work outside corners
- Yields 1" parallel hardwood edge

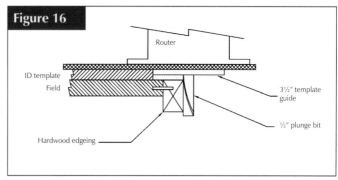

Figure 16

- Router
- ID template
- Field
- 3½" template guide
- ½" plunge bit
- Hardwood edgeing

Step 8. Inlay

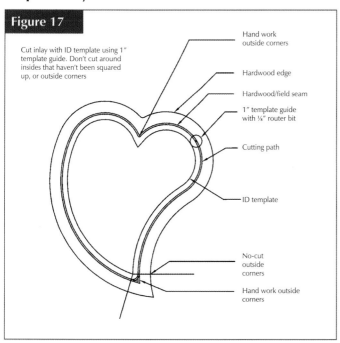

Figure 17

Cut inlay with ID template using 1" template guide. Don't cut around insides that haven't been squared up, or outside corners.

- Hand work outside corners
- Hardwood edge
- Hardwood/field seam
- 1" template guide with ⅛" router bit
- Cutting path
- ID template
- No-cut outside corners
- Hand work outside corners

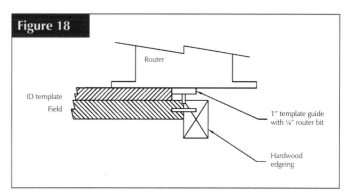

Figure 18

- Router
- ID template
- Field
- 1" template guide with ⅛" router bit
- Hardwood edgeing

Step: Alternate 1

1. Master pattern

2. Duplicate master pattern

3. ID template

4 & 5. Field and OD template (cut at same time)

6. Hardwood edge inside seam

7. Hardwood outside edge

8. Inlay

Step: Alternate 2

1. ID Template (make template ½" smaller than master pattern)

2 & 3. Field and OD template

4. Hardwood edge inside seam

5. Hardwood outside edge

6. Inlay

About the author

Scott Grove, an award-winning woodworker and member of the Furniture Society, has his work in leading museums and teaches across the US and in the UK. He maintains a studio in the Finger Lakes region of western New York, where he creates art furniture and sculpture. Grove is known for innovative techniques and an unconventional approach to furniture making.

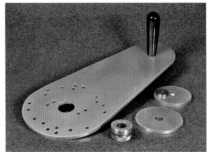

Universal extended router base and template guide bushings are available at imaginegrove.com.